COOKING WITH WINES AND SPIRITS

... AND BEER AND CIDER TOO

Cooking with Wines and Spirits

. . . and Beer and Cider too

by Elaine Hallgarten

Published by Hodder & Stoughton
in association with The Good Food Club

Cooking with Wines and Spirits is published by Hodder & Stoughton, 47 Bedford Square,
London WC1B 3DP in association with The Good Food Club, 14 Buckingham Street, London WC2N 6DS

ISBN 0 340 25056 9

Edited by Hilary Fawcett

Design by Theo Hodges/John Meek
Photographs by Norman Brand

Typesetting by Tradespools Limited, Frome, Somerset
Colour separations by Colourscreens Limited, Frome, Somerset

Printed and bound in England by
Hazell Watson & Viney, Aylesbury, Bucks

The publishers would like to thank
Berry Bros. and Rudd Ltd, James Burrough Ltd,
Café Royal, Rules Restaurant and Young & Co's
Brewery Ltd for allowing us to photograph
on their premises.

Also by Elaine Hallgarten:

Cookery Do (with Dorothy Brown) 1970
Fun Food and Facts (with Dorothy Brown) 1975
    (both published by Wine and Spirit Publications)
Mince Matters 1978 (Penguin)

Also from The Good Food Club:

The Good Food Guide Dinner Party Book (1971)
The Good Cook's Guide (1974)
The Good Food Guide Second Dinner Party Book (1979)

Contents

Introduction

Cooking wine, according to an old friend of mine, is the wine she drinks while she's cooking – which is certainly a novel definition. Personally I prefer my cooking wine in the pot, not out of it – and that goes for the cider, beer, spirits and liqueurs I use for cooking too. But, to adapt an old French saying, 'chacun à sa goutte', or 'each one to his drop'.

There's always been plenty of liquid other than water to enliven our cooking: all the different drinks that we splash (or carefully measure) into the stews and syllabubs, daubes and desserts, have a long and comforting history.

Beer

Britain has for centuries been a beer-drinking nation: ever since beer was first brewed in Anglo-Saxon times it has been 'top of the hops' from pubs to palaces. In the 14th century, Thames water was used in the brewing of ale in London. Queen Elizabeth I not only included strong ale in her breakfast menu but apparently regularly drank more during the day. Ale has been an important part of many festivals in the past, some of which still exist today – bride ale (bridal) is possibly the most famous. A less familiar audit ale, still brewed for Oxford colleges, was originally drunk on the day of the audit.

Cider

Cider too has been popular for hundreds of years, both in its rough, cloudy state and in the more modern crystal-clear and stabilised form. Its history is hidden in the mists of Celtic mythology when the apple was sacred and an apple god was worshipped. Primitive cider was made from the wild bitter apples of the forests. In the Middle Ages there was reference in monastic writings to cider, which became a substitute for French wines during the Hundred Years War. It was not until the end of the 19th century that cider-making began to be an industry rather than a cottage and farmhouse craft. There is a link, too, between cider and spirits, for in Normandy cider is used in the manufacture of calvados, which is a distilled apple brandy.

Wine

The Romans brought wine to Britain, even attempting to grow vines in our northerly climate, a relatively unsuccessful venture until the introduction of hardier strains which has recently made cultivation of vines a commercial proposition. The British wine trade has been importing the world's wines to our tables for centuries. Besides, one or two of France's vineyards are still English-owned. The greater interest in wine-drinking since the war, no doubt encouraged by wider travel, relative cheapness and a fashion for Continental styles of eating, allows Britain to boast today of a wine trade which covers all the markets of the world, from the great wines of Europe to the lesser-known ones from other continents.

Spirits and liqueurs

As for other drinks, while the English housewife was brewing beer, her Scottish counterpart was probably distilling whisky. In the Middle Ages every country lady had to know how to make liqueurs from fruit and spirit. Even in more recent times my grandmother and mother made their own cherry brandy – and some of my best friends produce delicious sloe gin.

Cooking with alcohol

With all this liquor around it is hardly surprising that a good deal of it has found its way into food. Certainly beer was used in Tudor cookery, as was cider. The Gauls had poured wine into their cooking-pots and the habit crossed the Channel. By 1710 a book on *Royal Cookery* by Patrick Lambe contained a recipe for salmon cooked in 'champaign wine', and Hannah Glasse, writing in the mid-18th century often used both wines and spirits to liven up her recipes. A contemporary of hers, Eliza Smith, combined ale with an 'old cock' to make a lethal-sounding drink: she prescribed pulverising the parboiled bird and immersing it in sack (sherry), adding raisins and spices and leaving it for nine days until it was bottled. A century later, on a more sophisticated note, Eliza Acton gave a recipe for truffles and sausages with madeira. Today the latter two ingredients are easy, but I fear truffles are beyond the reach of most of us.

Medicine

Another aspect of alcohol which nowadays is more of a music-hall joke than a reality is its use in medicine. This goes back at least to St Paul ('take a little wine for thy stomach's sake'). A book of Dorset folk remedies gives some fascinating recipes for brews to cure various ailments: 'For the gravel, boil a pint of milk, add half a pint of white wine, strain and add two ounces of marshmallows and two spoonfuls of salad oil – drink warm.' Another 18th-century hint to cure falling sickness: 'Quarter of a pint of white wine, grated nutmeg – pour down the throat of the victim.' And for a 'woman that cannot be delivered, after drinking the yolk of new-laid eggs, two pennyworth of saffron and sugar, she should drink mace ale or burnt claret.'

Vinegar

It may seem irrelevant to include vinegar here, but wine vinegar is a frequent ingredient in the ensuing recipes, and since it has very close ties with wine itself, it may not be so inappropriate. Not so long ago a friend told me that should I wish to make my own wine vinegar, I would need to acquire a 'mother' – a sort of skin that floats on the wine and through some chemical process turns it to vinegar. Shortly afterwards I mentioned my interest in wine vinegar to a friend in Burgundy. 'Would you like some of my mother?' he asked, in a friendly way. And so I travelled home, bearing in a screw-top jar, a part of his mother. Unfortunately the Customs officer didn't ask if I had anything to declare as I was hoping for the opportunity to tell him that I was carrying my friend's mother in a small jar. After several months my mother produced some fine, strong vinegar from the wine whose surface she floated on. On the Marne, incidentally, champagne vinegar is thought the ultimate in delicacy. In Britain, cider vinegar is useful – certainly if the alternative is malt.

Modern recipes

I do not consider cooking with wines, beers, and so on, either extravagant or ultra-sophisticated. 'It's all very well for her,' you may say, 'with access to plenty of wine.' Well, I confess to being in the fortunate position of having rather more wines and liqueurs to hand than the average housewife, thanks to a husband in the wine trade. And in that respect I have been lucky in having the benefit of his knowledge, as well as the remains of innumerable wine-tastings. But if you study the economics of cooking with alcohol, you do not need a computer to tell you that the cost of the liquid addition to any given dish is generally a relatively small proportion of the total expenditure. This proportion has become smaller rather than greater in recent years, with the spiralling cost of food and the comparatively stable cost of alcoholic drinks.

Although it might appear that using a drop of wine, or beer, or cider puts your cooking into the 'for guests only' bracket, I would urge you to consider it a normal everyday matter to add a little something to family food as well. All the recipes in this book have pleased the critical palates of my own family and I have not felt I have been pushing my dear ones on the road to alcoholism by introducing them to the joys of food cooked with a few spoonsful of wine. As most readers will know, the very cooking drives off the alcohol and you are left with the flavour of the original ingredients, transformed by fermentation or distillation. Again, the difference in taste between red and white wines is not only a question of colour and grape variety. Red wines contain extra flavour derived from the grape pips and stalks during fermentation, and add their own complex tastes to the food.

The flavour of distilled spirits is mainly volatile, and much of it disappears along with the spirit during cooking. What remains, though, is highly concentrated. Sweet liqueurs, on the other hand, will lose their alcohol in the cooking process while most of the flavour and sugar remain. Beer loses its alcohol but is so low in strength that there is not much change in the concentration of flavours. It does however lose its particularly beery flavour (a fact which I as a non-beer drinker discovered to my delight). The flavours from the beer give the finished dish an extra delicious complexity, as you will learn if you try some of the beer recipes. Cooking with cider concentrates the original apple flavour, which harmonises with other appropriately-chosen ingredients in the dish. Flambé dishes are usually associated with restaurants, and extravagance in all senses, but the technique does not have to be confined to crêpes Suzette. Many recipes are more digestible because of the spoonful of spirit that has been warmed, ignited, and poured over at some stage of the cooking, to burn off surplus fat and leave an aromatic flavour behind.

In some recipes the spirit, wine, or whatever, may not be cooked and therefore you will be imbibing the product, alcohol and all. But generally in these instances only a fairly small quantity is required.

Quantity

This raises the vital point of quantity. It may be difficult to believe, but the truth about alcohol and food is that you don't necessarily improve your recipe by increasing the amount of liquor you add to the dish. In fact you might actually spoil it. So if a recipe says two tablespoonsful of the specified spirit, that is what you should use – not four on the basis that it will make the finished dish twice as good. With sweet wines remember that the sweetness will remain in the completed dish.

Quality

From quantity to quality, and here there are vast areas of difference. Many schools of thought insist that you should cook with the finest wines and spirits, suggesting that a glassful or two from the old Château Lafite will scarcely be missed and the odd spoonful of V.S.O.P. cognac is as essential in the kitchen as in your best cut-glass decanter. Well, good luck to those who can afford such thoughts (and deeds). For my own culinary ambitions I have always contented myself with using whatever odds and ends I've had available. When I have had to open a new bottle of wine for cooking, I have used a good, sound plonk of whatever variety the recipe called for. Similarly with sherry – a well-made Cyprus sherry or best British sherry has provided many a *dosage* to my bubbling pots and casseroles. When brandy is what I specify in my recipes, brandy is what I use (except in dire emergencies when the household's best cognac has been sacrificed).

However, as I have said, there are different ideas about this subject, and who am I to stop you pouring your most prized claret into a beef stew, or your highly esteemed Riesling into cod fingers au vin blanc? Perhaps the truth is, though, that if like any Burgundian you think there is a real difference between coq au Chambertin and coq au Marocain, you had better take as much trouble over the coq as you spend money on the bottle. But even in Burgundy it is highly unlikely that *le vrai* Chambertin will accompany the coq.

A natural sequel to the question of quality is the life-expectancy of opened bottles. With beer and cider it isn't usually a problem, as the remains of a bottle or can may be speedily despatched without great expense down the nearest thirsty throat. Spirits and liqueurs obviously have a long life in opened bottles or decanters, and fortified wines such as sherry, madeira and port will also keep their flavour for a long time. But if you have a fair amount of wine left, you should guard it zealously. You may care to decant it into a smaller bottle, stoppering it securely to keep it free from air. I confess to being lazy and tending to leave the wines in their original bottles. They survive a great deal longer than most people would believe, and I never throw away anything without verifying its usefulness. I would certainly not pour wine into a dish without first checking that it is sound – basically, non-vinegary. Contrary to generally held views, I keep remnants of wines for months, and more often than not I find they are quite usable. This applies to red and white wines, kept well corked and in a pantry or cool cupboard – the whites if possible in the refrigerator. There is no reason why you should not combine compatible wines or use odd drops to top up your vinegar bottle.

Keeping a half-empty bottle of wine isn't going to improve it, but if you are prepared to give the odd opened bottle house room, I think it is well worth hanging onto everything, however little is left. A half-glass of wine can make a very ordinary bolognese sauce that much nicer or a chicken casserole far more interesting. A small quantity of wine added to the pan juices after frying meat provides a sauce for steak or hamburgers, veal or poultry. The last few drops in a bottle of wine, sherry, madeira or port need never be wasted. The odd spoonful of muscatel added to vegetables has delightful results. In the same economical vein, you can whisk a very small quantity of liqueur into cream to be served with fresh fruit.

The recipes

While upholding the admirable advice proffered in *The Good Food Guide Dinner Party Book* and its sequels, I have borne in mind that this book is different from its predecessors in that the recipes are not from a restaurant kitchen but from a domestic one. I have therefore offered occasional short-cuts and ingredients which might be frowned upon by professional chefs or restaurant critics but which I think are justified in the hurly-burly of a home. I have tried to use ingredients which are for the most part readily available, and not too expensive, hence the omission of frogs' legs, wild boar and truffles, which no longer warrant a place in a book of this nature.

The recipes in the book are sufficient for four to six – the variation allows for a gluttonous four or a more abstemious five or six. Where there is any doubt, I have specified the number precisely.

Basic recipes are given at the end of the book. Eggs are, unless otherwise stated, size three. Spoons are all level. As is usual nowadays, metric and imperial measures are given, but you should use either all metric or all imperial – do not mix the two. You may prefer to use double or whipping cream instead of all or some of the single cream in sauces. I have used single because I find double cream unnecessarily rich and this is, if you like, a small attempt at economy of both calories and cost.

The wine table (page 14) and the liqueurs and spirits table (page 15) will, I hope, be helpful in deciding how best to use what you have available. Cider and beer obviously do not require such detailed descriptions.

Always remember that no recipe is sacrosanct – it is your individual touch which makes it come to life and gives your cooking flair.

Acknowledgements

I would like to thank the many friends, especially those in the wine and spirit trade, who gave me help with recipes and advice, and particularly the following: Friedel Hallgarten for family recipes; Barbara and Bep Salvi for Italian recipes; Bardinet; Lucas Bols; The Brewers Society; British Poultry Information Service; British Sausage Bureau; Bulmers Cider; de Kuyper; Merrydown Vineyards Ltd; Stock's Distilleries Ltd; Syndicat National des Industries Cydricoles; Wine Development Board. My grateful thanks are due to my editor, Hilary Fawcett, for her patient help and constant encouragement.

Finally, my love and thanks to my husband Peter, who has contributed immeasurably with his expertise, his enthusiasm, and – not least – his huge appetite.

Wine table

The following table indicates, in general terms, the various types of wines which are likely to be found in off-licences and supermarkets. In the recipes I have, for simplicity's sake, suggested wines as follows: red; full-bodied red; dry white; fruity white; sweet white; rosé. Other wines, found in the table under 'Miscellaneous' are referred to in the book as follows: sherry dry/medium/sweet; madeira dry/sweet; port white/tawny/ruby; marsala. A rough guide to prices is that the wines are listed in order of expense, with the least expensive first in each category. The recipes work well with whatever I have prescribed, but there is, as you can see, a wider range from which to choose and it obviously depends on what you have available.

TYPE OF WINE	WINES AVAILABLE
RED	
Light (claret)	Vins de table (French/Italian); vins de pays; Dāo
Full (claret)	Argentine; Chilean; Rioja; Chianti; California; Bordeaux
Soft (burgundy)	Australian; Midi; South African; red Loire; Beaujolais
FULL-BODIED RED	
Full (burgundy)	Rhône; red burgundy
DRY WHITE	
Light dry	Yugoslav; Austrian; Moselle/Rhine; white Bordeaux; champagne
Full dry	Spanish; Soave; Pouilly Fumé/Sancerre; Rhône; Chablis; burgundy
FRUITY WHITE	
Medium dry light	Verdicchio; Vouvray; German Kabinett/Spätlese; Alsace; sparkling wines from Germany/France/Spain
SWEET WHITE	
Medium sweet	Coteaux du Layon; German Auslese
Sweet	Sauternes/Barsac; sweet Muscat; Asti Spumante
ROSÉ	
Dry	Provence; Tavel
Medium	Anjou; Portuguese; pink Champagne
MISCELLANEOUS	British sherry; Cyprus sherry; sherry (dry/medium/sweet)
	Vermouth white/red/bianco
	Madeira dry/sweet
	Port white/tawny/ruby
	Marsala

Liqueurs and spirits table

Liqueurs and spirits are classified into general groups according to their main flavour. Where liqueurs or spirits are called for I have given alternatives in the recipe where appropriate but a fuller choice will be found here. Brandy is perfectly acceptable for cooking but if you prefer cognac, by all means use it. Liqueurs and spirits are listed in alphabetical not price order. Many liqueur houses publish their own attractive and helpful booklets with recipes. If you like cooking with liqueurs as well as drinking them, do send for these publications, which are invariably free.

MAIN FLAVOUR	LIQUEURS, SPIRITS, EAUX-DE-VIE
Whisky liqueur	Drambuie; Glayva; Glen Mist
Herb	Bénédictine; Chartreuse; Galliano; Izarra; Strega
Seed	Anis/Anisette; aquavit; kümmel; ouzo; Pernod
Mint	Crème-de-Menthe; Pippermint; Royal Mint-Chocolate
Citrus	Cointreau; Curaçao; Filfar; Grand Marnier; Mandarine Napoléon; Nassau Orange; Sabra; Van der Hum
Apricot/peach	Amaretto; apricot brandy; peach brandy
Cherry	Cherry brandy; Cherry Heering
Miscellaneous fruits	Crème de Cassis; sloe gin
Coffee	Kahlúa; Royal French; Tia Maria
Chocolate	Crème de Cacao; Royal Liqueurs (Ginger-Chocolate; Lemon-Chocolate; Orange-Chocolate)
Fruit spirits	Calvados; kirsch; quetsch; slivovitz; tequila; Eau-de-vie de Framboise; Eau-de-vie de Poire (Poire Williams)
White spirits	Gin; white rum; vodka
Grape spirits	Armagnac; brandy; cognac
Cereal spirits	American whiskey; Irish whiskey; Scotch whisky
Rum	Various British brands; Negrita

Soups

In the age of convenience foods, a home-made soup is a sure sign of a caring cook – but anyone who makes her/his own soups knows that any effort involved is easily outweighed by the pleasure it brings.

As my family has the reputation for being eccentrically enthusiastic about soups (two members are known to order soups for dessert in restaurants, much to the amazement of the waiters) I am used to making enormous quantities, hoping to freeze some, only to find the tureen empty. If you have a less gluttonous family, it is well worth making double or more of a recipe and freezing half for another meal.

Stock freezes well too and recipes are given on page 214 for making your own. It goes without saying that home-made soups based on good stock are the perfect formula. However, if you choose to take a short-cut (and I often do), use the readily available stock cubes, go easy on the seasoning, and be prepared for a more uniform taste to your efforts. Do buy the best (and probably most expensive) stock cubes as the cheaper ones do not have a very satisfactory flavour.

The addition of a small shot of liquor can enhance the simplest of bouillons. At the other end of the scale, a true bouillabaisse has almost as much wine in it as fish stock. If you are using wine to pep up your soup, you will probably choose a dry sherry or madeira, fortified wines being best suited to the task.

Jellied Bloody Mary

A more solid version of a popular drink – this soup looks as attractive as it sounds, and tastes even better.

five 5 ml spoons	gelatine	5 teasp
three 15 ml spoons	water	3 tablesp
300 ml	chicken stock (page 215)	½ pint
600 ml	tomato juice	1 pint
four 15 ml spoons	vodka	4 tablesp
150 ml	sour cream	¼ pint
six 5 ml spoons	black lumpfish roe (mock caviar)	6 teasp

Soften the gelatine in the cold water. Heat the stock and stir in the softened gelatine until it is dissolved. Strain it onto the tomato juice. Stir in the vodka.

Rinse a shallow dish (a roasting-tin would do) with cold water and then pour in the mixture. Leave it to set, for a minimum of three hours, in the refrigerator. Roughly chop the set jelly and spoon it into individual glasses (a champagne glass is ideal). Put a spoonful of sour cream on top of each and then some lumpfish roe in the centre of the sour cream.

Serve well chilled. The jelly does not become very firm.

If no vodka is available, use another spirit, such as aquavit or kümmel.

Fruit soup

1 kg	plums	2 lb
three 15 ml spoons	brown sugar	3 tablesp
1.25 litres	water	2 pints
300 ml	red wine	½ pint
one	small stick of cinnamon	one
one 15 ml spoon	cornflour	1 tablesp

Wash the plums and remove the stalks. Put everything except the cornflour into a large pan and bring it to the boil. Reduce the heat, cover the pan and simmer it until the fruit is cooked. Rub the stewed fruit through a sieve and return it to the pan. Taste for sweetness and add more sugar if required. (Remember that chilled liquids need more sugar than hot.)

Mix the cornflour with a little cold water and stir it into the fruit. Cook the soup over a gentle heat for a few minutes to thicken it slightly. Pour it into a bowl and leave it to cool before refrigerating it, overnight if possible.

Use any fruit you like, or a mixture of fruits. Cherries, peaches and apricots are particularly good, but apples and pears could be added.

Cold cucumber and salmon soup

You can take advantage of reasonable prices at the fishmonger's to tuck a little salmon into the freezer for use in this soup.

ten	*spring onions*	*ten*
40 g	*butter*	*1½ oz*
25 g	*cornflour*	*1 oz*
600 ml	*fish stock (page 215)*	*1 pint*
two	*cucumbers*	*two*
two 15 ml spoons	*lemon juice*	*2 tablesp*
150 ml	*dry white wine*	*¼ pint*
	salt, pepper	
225 g	*salmon or salmon trout*	*½ lb*
150 ml	*single cream*	*¼ pint*

Chop the onions, including a little of the green part, and soften them in the butter. Stir in the cornflour. Gradually add the stock, stirring constantly. Cook the mixture for a few minutes. Peel and thinly slice the cucumber, reserving a few slices for garnishing the soup. Add the remainder to the pan, together with the lemon juice, wine, salt and pepper. Bring the contents of the pan to the boil, cover it and simmer for 15 minutes.

Add the salmon and poach it for 15 minutes. Take the salmon from the liquid and remove the skin and bones. Flake the fish and reserve it. Liquidise the soup. Add the flaked fish and cool the soup before refrigerating it for several hours.

Stir in the cream, and serve the soup with the reserved cucumber slices floating on top.

Chestnut soup

Tinned chestnut puree is the answer to a lazy cook's prayer. While it may not be as good as the real thing, it enables you to conjure up the taste of chestnuts without the agony of peeling them. If you prefer the true flavour, make a puree of fresh chestnuts, and proceed . . .

one	*large onion*	*one*
three	*sticks of celery*	*three*
25 g	*butter*	*1 oz*
450 g	*unsweetened chestnut puree*	*1 lb*
1 litre	*chicken stock (page 215)*	*1¾ pints*
125 ml	*dry madeira*	*4 fl oz*
three 15 ml spoons	*double cream*	*3 tablesp*

Soften the finely-chopped onion and celery in the butter. Add the chestnut puree, stirring to soften it. Add the chicken stock and cook the mixture, covered, over a moderate heat for 20 minutes. Liquidise the soup and return it to the pan. Add the madeira and cream and warm them through.

If you prefer a thicker soup, add some beurre manié (page 216).

Chicken curry soup

Cold curry may seem a contradiction in terms but it makes a refreshing summer soup. Use genuine, well-flavoured chicken stock for this recipe.

one	*medium-sized onion*	*one*
50 g	*butter*	*2 oz*
two 15 ml spoons	*curry powder*	*2 tablesp*
40 g	*flour*	*1½ oz*
600 ml	*chicken stock (page 215)*	*1 pint*
450 ml	*milk*	*¾ pint*
150 ml	*cream*	*¼ pint*
150 ml	*sweet sherry*	*¼ pint*

Soften the chopped onion in the butter. Stir in the curry powder and cook it for three minutes. Remove the pan from the heat and add the flour. Slowly add the stock, stirring constantly. Return the pan to the heat and stir the contents until you have a smooth mixture. Cook it for ten minutes. Liquidise the soup with the milk and cream. Stir in the sherry and leave it to cool.

Refrigerate the soup and serve it cold, with a little more cream if desired.

Majorcan vegetable soup

This substantial soup would make an excellent supper party main course, with a hearty pudding to follow. The lack of meat stock will appeal to vegetarians.

three 15 ml spoons	*olive oil*	*3 tablesp*
six	*cloves of garlic*	*six*
two	*large Spanish onions*	*two*
50 g	*cauliflower*	*2 oz*
225 g	*tomatoes*	*½ lb*
one	*small red pepper*	*one*
one	*small green pepper*	*one*
1.75 litres	*hot water*	*3 pints*
one	*heart of a small white cabbage*	*one*
two 15 ml spoons	*chopped parsley*	*2 tablesp*
one	*bay leaf*	*one*
	salt, pepper	
two	*slices of stale bread*	*two*
300 ml	*dry white wine*	*½ pint*

Heat the oil in a heavy saucepan and add the crushed garlic, and the chopped onions and cauliflower. Cook the vegetables gently for ten minutes, stirring occasionally. Add the peeled and sliced tomatoes and the sliced peppers. Cook for a further 15 minutes, stirring occasionally. Add the hot water and bring it to the boil. Add the finely-chopped cabbage, the parsley and bay leaf. Season very well and simmer the soup, covered, for 1½ hours. Break the bread into very small pieces and add it to the soup. Cook the soup for a further five minutes. Stir in the wine, warm it through and serve immediately.

Add other vegetables, according to what you have at hand.

Ham and lentil soup

700 g–1 kg	*gammon hock or knuckle*	*1½–2 lb*
one	*large onion*	*one*
one	*carrot*	*one*
one	*stick of celery*	*one*
one	*bay leaf*	*one*
six	*peppercorns*	*six*
225 g	*dried lentils*	*½ lb*
450 ml	*brown ale*	*¾ pint*
	salt, pepper	

Place the hock in a large pan with the peeled and chopped vegetables, the bay leaf and the peppercorns, and cover them with water. Bring it to the boil, cover the pan, and cook the contents for about three hours, until the meat is falling off the bone. (Pressure-cook for one hour.) Meanwhile cover the lentils with boiling water and soak them for at least two hours.

Strain the liquid from the hock and measure 1 litre (1¾ pints) into a saucepan. Add the drained lentils. Cut the ham from the bone and chop it into small pieces. Add it to the stock and lentils, together with the vegetables from the stock if you wish. Add the ale. Cook for a further two hours (pressure-cook for 50 minutes). Check the seasoning.

Cream of onion soup

1 kg	*onions*	*2 lb*
two	*cloves of garlic*	*two*
50 g	*butter*	*2 oz*
600 ml	*veal or chicken stock (page 215)*	*1 pint*
600 ml	*dark ale*	*1 pint*
150 ml	*single cream*	*¼ pint*
four	*egg yolks*	*four*
	salt, pepper	

Soften the thinly-sliced onions and crushed garlic in the hot butter until they are golden. Add the stock and ale, cover, and cook the soup for 15 minutes.

Liquidise the soup, slowly adding the cream and beaten yolks. Reheat gently and season.

French onion soup

Most recipes for onion soup seem to be rather mean with the onions. I like mine to be a lot of onions and a little soup.

40 g	butter	1½ oz
one 15 ml spoon	olive oil	1 tablesp
1 kg	onions	2 lb
one 15 ml spoon	brown sugar	1 tablesp
two 15 ml spoons	flour	2 tablesp
	salt, pepper	
1.75 litres	beef stock (page 214)	3 pints
300 ml	dry white wine	½ pint
six	slices of French bread	six
175 g	grated hard cheese	6 oz

Heat the butter and oil. Add the thinly-sliced onions and stir them round to coat them well. Cover and cook for 15 minutes, stirring from time to time. When the onions are golden brown, stir in the sugar, flour, salt and pepper. Mix everything well and then add the stock and wine. Bring it to the boil, reduce the heat and simmer, covered, for 45 minutes.

Toast the French bread. Pour the soup into an oven-proof dish. Float the toasted bread on top and scatter the cheese over it. Grill for five minutes to melt the cheese and brown it a little.

This soup is much improved if made the day before, but in that case, of course, add the bread and cheese only when you have reheated it.

Cream of fennel soup with Pernod

This is a lusciously thick soup in which the subtle flavour of fennel is enhanced by the addition of Pernod.

two	*medium-sized onions*	*two*
	oil or butter	
700 g (approx.)	*Florentine fennel*	*1½ lb (approx.)*
350 ml	*veal or chicken stock (page 215)*	*12 fl oz*
350 ml	*milk*	*12 fl oz*
	salt, pepper	
150 ml	*single cream*	*¼ pint*
two 15 ml spoons	*Pernod*	*2 tablesp*

Soften the thinly-sliced onions in the oil. Roughly chop the fennel and add it to the onions. Stir it round and cook it for five minutes. Add the stock, milk, salt and pepper. Bring the soup to the boil and simmer it, covered, for about 30 minutes, or until the fennel is soft. Liquidise the soup and return it to the heat. Stir in the cream and Pernod and warm the soup gently.

Cream of parsnip soup

Parsnips are either loved or loathed. For the lovers, this is a thick and very parsnippy-flavoured soup, with a wee dram for extra warmth.

one	*medium-sized onion*	*one*
	butter	
450 g	*parsnips*	*1 lb*
1 litre	*chicken stock (page 215)*	*1¾ pints*
600 ml	*milk*	*1 pint*
	salt, pepper	
two 15 ml spoons	*whisky*	*2 tablesp*

Soften the chopped onion in the hot butter. Add the peeled and diced parsnips and stir them round for a few minutes. Add the stock, cover, and cook the soup until the parsnips are very soft. (Pressure-cooking takes only eight minutes.) Liquidise the soup, adding the milk. Return the liquidised soup to the pan and re-heat, adding salt and pepper. Just before serving, stir in the whisky.

Fish soup

Perhaps no other recipe so deserves a place in this collection, for it is very extravagant in its use of wine. But the convenient thing about it is that you can use up any odds and ends of sound white wine to make up the quantity required since the flavour of the fish will certainly disguise any variation in the wine. The other attractions of fish soup are that if you prefer to make a stew out of it, you can add more fish, and you can use almost any combination of fish you choose. The suggestions I make are for those I find most easily obtainable, but your fishmonger might be able to recommend different varieties.

one	*small red mullet*	*one*
one	*small whiting*	*one*
175 g	*cod fillet*	*6 oz*
one	*small mackerel*	*one*
one	*small gurnet (gurnard)*	*one*
110 g	*peeled prawns*	*1/4 lb*
one 15 ml spoon	*olive oil*	*1 tablesp*
two	*medium-sized onions*	*two*
two	*leeks*	*two*
225 g	*tomatoes*	*1/2 lb*
one	*large clove of garlic*	*one*
one	*bouquet garni (page 216)*	*one*
	salt, pepper	
1 litre	*fish stock (page 215)*	*1 3/4 pints*
450 ml	*dry white wine*	*3/4 pint*
	chopped parsley	

Prepare the fish: remove the heads and tails and fillet the fish, or ask the fishmonger to do this for you. Cut the fish into small pieces. Peel the prawns if necessary. Use all the trimmings and the shells of the prawns for the stock. Heat the oil in a large pan and soften the sliced onions and leeks (white part only) for a few minutes. Add the peeled, seeded and chopped tomatoes, the crushed garlic, bouquet garni, salt and pepper. Stir the mixture well. Pour in the stock and wine, bring them to the boil, and simmer for ten minutes. Add the prepared fish and keep the soup simmering for a further 15 minutes. Add the chopped parsley five minutes before serving.

Garlic croûtons are often served with this soup. If you wanted to give it a touch of the bouillabaisse you could serve it with a garlicky mayonnaise or special sauce known as rouille. The Marseillais also pass around grated cheese with their fish soup. Another possibility is to thicken the soup with beurre manié (page 216). I don't think any of these extras are necessary (except the croûtons) if the soup is good and full of flavour. As with many soups, this one improves on re-heating.

Cream of tomato soup

Tomato and orange soup is not unknown so why not exchange the orange for an orange liqueur?

one	*medium-sized onion*	*one*
	oil	
400 g	*tinned tomatoes*	*14 oz*
one 15 ml spoon	*tomato puree*	*1 tablesp*
225 g	*carrots*	*½ lb*
1 litre	*chicken stock (page 215)*	*1¾ pints*
	salt, pepper	
three 15 ml spoons	*orange liqueur*	*3 tablesp*

Soften the sliced onion in the oil. Add the tomatoes, tomato puree, sliced carrots, stock, salt and pepper. Bring the soup to the boil and then simmer for 25 minutes. Liquidise or sieve the soup and return it to the pan. Warm it through and, just before serving, add the liqueur.

You can increase the richness of the soup by adding some cream when re-heating it. Do not allow it to boil.

Wine soup

Wine soup is delicate and depends as much on the flavour of the wine as on the good stock.

1 litre	*chicken stock (page 215)*	*1¾ pints*
450 ml	*dry white wine*	*¾ pints*
four	*egg yolks*	*four*
one 5 ml spoon	*sugar*	*1 teasp*
	salt, pepper	
50 g	*rice, cooked*	*2 oz*

Heat the stock with the wine until it begins to boil. Beat the egg yolks and add the hot liquid drop by drop, beating constantly. Return the mixture to the pan and heat it very gently. Do not allow it to boil. Add the sugar, salt and pepper, and the cooked rice. Stir well and simmer the soup over a very gentle heat (or in a double-boiler) to warm the rice.

Smoked haddock bisque

If you keep a supply of smoked haddock in the freezer, this soup can be produced in no time at all.

450 g	*smoked haddock fillets*	*1 lb*
600 ml	*water*	*1 pint*
600 ml	*dry white wine*	*1 pint*
one	*slice of onion*	*one*
one	*small carrot*	*one*
one	*stick of celery*	*one*
	pepper	
40 g	*butter*	*1½ oz*
40 g	*flour*	*1½ oz*
150 ml	*single cream*	*¼ pint*
three 15 ml spoons	*whisky*	*3 tablesp*

Poach the fish in the water and wine, along with the onion, sliced carrot, chopped celery and a little pepper. Make a roux (page 217) with the butter and flour and when the fish is cooked, strain the liquid onto the roux and mix it to a smooth sauce. Cook it for five minutes. Flake the fish and liquidise it with the sauce until it is quite smooth. Add the cream and reheat the soup gently. Stir in the whisky just before serving.

Hors d'oeuvre and vegetables

The *Dictionary of Gastronomy* defines hors d'oeuvre as 'easy-to-take foods, hot or cold, served before a meal or before the main part of the meal. They can be of any and every kind but ideally they are light and tempting – stimulating the palate without clogging it or dulling the appetite.'

I think that is a most excellent definition, to which I would make only two exceptions – that some of the recipes in this section would make a meal in themselves, albeit lightweight, and others might be suited to being part of a cold buffet. Indeed a wine and pâté party would make a pleasant change from the old favourite of wine and cheese.

Generally speaking, I don't find that vegetables and alcohol make a particularly happy marriage, but there are a few that work well.

Eggs and cheese, pâtés and pastas, fish and fruit – all are represented in this hotchpotch of recipes.

Grapefruit and Pernod sorbet

A wonderfully fresh start to a meal, this tingling ice needs to be served direct from the freezer, preferably to waiting guests, for it melts very quickly. It is equally delicious as a palate-cleanser between courses or as a final course.

75 g	sugar	3 oz
150 ml	water	¼ pint
two	large grapefruit	two
three 15 ml spoons	Pernod	3 tablesp
one	egg white	one

Make a syrup with the sugar and water, cook it for ten minutes, and leave it to cool. Peel the grapefruit, removing all the pith. Cut the fruit into chunks. Remove the pips.

Liquidise the grapefruit with the cooled syrup until you have a rather rough sauce (it is very difficult to puree the grapefruit). Stir in the Pernod and when the mixture is completely cold, place it in the freezer for a minimum of eight hours, preferably overnight.

When the mixture has frozen solid, remove it from the freezer and soften it with a fork. Whisk the egg white until it is very stiff and gently fold it into the softened ice. Blend the mixture in the liquidiser for a minute or two until it is light and smooth. Return it to the freezer for a further six hours, or more if possible.

A short time before you want to serve the sorbet, place four to six glasses in the freezer to chill them. With an ice-cream scoop, or a spoon, make balls of the sorbet and place them on a plate in the freezer. When your guests are sitting down, pop a ball of sorbet into each glass and serve it, decorated, if you wish, with a previously-prepared twist of grapefruit peel or a sprig of fennel.

You can make this sorbet with gin, whisky or kümmel. Remember that Pernod is perhaps the most strongly-flavoured spirit and aniseed is not to everyone's taste.

Rosé grapefruit

The secret of this deliciously simple recipe is the cardamom, a little of which goes a long way. Crush the seeds from inside the pods. Use a fruity white wine instead of the rosé if you wish.

four 15 ml spoons	*clear honey*	*4 tablesp*
three 15 ml spoons	*water*	*3 tablesp*
one	*pinch of cardamom*	*one*
125 ml	*rosé wine*	*4 fl oz*
three	*grapefruit*	*three*

Put the honey, water and cardamom into a pan and bring them to the boil; reduce the heat and simmer for five minutes. Add the wine and leave the liquid to cool. Peel the grapefruit, remove all the pith and slice the fruit thinly. Remove the pips. Put the fruit into a bowl and pour over the syrup (strained if you wish). Refrigerate until required. Serve the grapefruit very cold.

Melon cocktail

We are fortunate in having melons almost all the year round, so when we tire of having them unadorned, we can always liven them up with a glassful of wine or spirit.

one	*large melon*	*one*
three 15 ml spoons	*red vermouth*	*3 tablesp*

Either cut the melon into small pieces or scoop out the flesh with a melon-baller. Put the cut-up melon into a bowl and pour over the vermouth. Keep it in the refrigerator, covered, until it is required.

The Provencal way with melons gives you a drink as well as the fruit to eat. Take a water-melon and cut off the top. Scoop out as many seeds as possible and fill the cavity with a Tavel Rosé or Châteauneuf-du-Pape red wine. Replace the lid and refrigerate the melon for several hours. Pour the wine through a sieve into a jug and serve it immediately. Slice the melon and eat it with the wine.

A sweet white wine could be used instead, or sherry, port, madeira, or a more spirited liquid such as brandy or anis.

Cold courgette salad

All too often salad means lettuce, cucumber and tomatoes. This is a pleasant alternative.

one	small onion	one
one	small carrot	one
25 g	butter	1 oz
150 ml	water	¼ pint
150 ml	dry white wine	¼ pint
two	cloves of garlic	two
one	bouquet garni (page 216)	one
	salt, pepper	
700 g	courgettes	1½ lb

Put the finely-chopped onion and carrot in a pan with the butter, water, wine, crushed garlic, bouquet garni, salt and pepper. Bring the mixture to the boil, cover the pan, and simmer it for ten minutes.

Cut the unpeeled courgettes into 1-cm (½-inch) slices and add them to the pan. Simmer them, covered, until they are just tender. Transfer them, with the sauce, to a dish, leave it to cool, and refrigerate. Serve the courgettes as part of an hors d'oeuvre or as a salad.

Leeks in rosé wine

Serve the leeks as an accompaniment to a grill, or even on their own as a first course with garlic bread.

1.25 kg	leeks	2½ lb
50 g	butter	2 oz
25 g	flour	1 oz
300 ml	rosé wine	½ pint
	salt, pepper	

Trim and discard the green part of the leeks; wash them well and slice them. Cook the leeks in butter for five minutes, stirring from time to time. Remove the pan from the heat and stir in the flour. Add the wine and seasoning and return to a very low heat for 40 minutes (or cook the leeks in the oven if it is already on).

Marrons au vin blanc

My passion for chestnuts is usually somewhat dimmed by the prospect of having to peel a quantity of them, but the labour is amply rewarded by the end product.

1 kg	chestnuts	2 lb
175 g	streaky bacon	6 oz
	butter	
225 g	button onions	½ lb
300 ml	dry white wine	½ pint
150 ml	water	¼ pint
	salt, pepper	

Make a slit in the chestnuts, put them in a pan and cover them with water. Bring the water to the boil, cover the pan, and simmer the chestnuts for ten minutes. Drain the water off and peel the chestnuts, removing the inner skin. It doesn't matter if they are broken but try to have a few whole ones.

Brown the chopped bacon in a little butter. Add the peeled onions and brown them well. Add the peeled chestnuts. Cover them with the wine and water, add salt and pepper, and bring the mixture to the boil. Cover the pan and simmer it for about 45 minutes, or until the chestnuts are tender. Check from time to time that there is plenty of liquid and if necessary top it up in the same proportions of wine to water. By the end of the cooking most of the liquid should be absorbed. Serve with roast meat or poultry.

Mushrooms in vermouth

one	small onion	one
50 g	butter	2 oz
450 g	button mushrooms	1 lb
	salt, pepper	
two 15 ml spoons	brandy	2 tablesp
100 ml	red vermouth	3 fl oz
125 ml	single cream	4 fl oz
	fresh herbs	

Soften the finely-chopped onion in the butter. Add the sliced mushrooms and cook them for a few minutes just to soften them. Season them well.

Warm the brandy in a soup ladle, ignite it and pour it over the mushrooms. When the flames subside, pour on the vermouth and cook it until the liquid has reduced by about half. Add the cream and more salt and pepper if necessary. Sprinkle on some finely-chopped fresh herbs.

Serve hot, in small pots, or on toast, or as a vol-au-vent filling.

Stuffed mushrooms

Stuffing mushrooms seems a little fiddly, but this dish can be prepared in advance and finished off at the last moment.

twelve	*large flat mushrooms*	*twelve*
	olive oil	
50 g	*streaky bacon*	*2 oz*
one	*small onion*	*one*
	salt, pepper	
one	*egg*	*one*
two 15 ml spoons	*single cream*	*2 tablesp*
one 15 ml spoon	*brandy*	*1 tablesp*
two 15 ml spoons	*fine breadcrumbs*	*2 tablesp*

Carefully remove the stems of the mushrooms and reserve them. Wipe the mushrooms and brush them with a little oil. Place them on a baking-sheet and bake them in a hot oven (220°C, 425°F, mark 7) for five minutes.

Toss the finely-chopped bacon and onion in the oil, together with the reserved mushroom stems, chopped. Cook this mixture gently for ten minutes. Season to taste. Beat the egg, cream and brandy together and add them to the pan, stirring well. Remove the pan from the heat.

Put the mushrooms on a grill-pan lined with foil. Pile the stuffing mixture in the mushroom cups. Scatter the breadcrumbs on top and drizzle a little oil over each one. Brown them under the grill.

Marinated mushrooms

one	small onion	one
one	clove of garlic	one
two 15 ml spoons	chopped parsley	2 tablesp
one 5 ml spoon	fresh tarragon	1 teasp
	(or half quantity dried)	
150 ml	dry white wine	¼ pint
50 ml	white wine vinegar	2 fl oz
50 ml	olive oil	2 fl oz
one 15 ml spoon	lemon juice	1 tablesp
one	bay leaf	one
	salt, pepper	
450 g	very small button mushrooms	1 lb

Liquidise all the ingredients except the bay leaf, salt, pepper and mushrooms until the onion is pureed. Pour the mixture into a saucepan and add the bay leaf, salt and pepper. Bring the mixture to the boil and simmer it for three minutes. Wipe the mushrooms and pour the hot sauce over them. Leave them to cool before refrigerating for 2–3 hours.

Serve them as part of an hors d'oeuvre or on their own with hot garlic bread.

Melanzane a scapece

Serve this aubergine dish as a salad or as a pickle with cold meats.

four	large aubergines	four
	salt	
300 ml	dry white wine	½ pint
300 ml	red wine vinegar	½ pint
twelve	mint leaves	twelve
three	cloves of garlic	three
one	dried chilli pepper	one

Remove the ends of the aubergines, wash and dry them and cut them into 2.5-cm (one-inch) cubes, without peeling them. Salt them well and leave them for one hour. Rinse the aubergine pieces and put them into a casserole with the wine and vinegar. If necessary add a little water so that the liquid just covers the aubergines. Add the mint, the crushed garlic and the crumbled chilli. Bring the mixture to the boil and cook it for about 15 minutes – the aubergines should remain firm.

Transfer the contents of the pan to a bowl to cool and then refrigerate it until required. This will keep in sealed jars for several weeks in the refrigerator.

Petits oignons

The only drawback to this lovely spicy dish is having to peel all the onions, but once that is done your problems are over. The easiest way is to plunge them briefly first into boiling water and then into cold.

700 g	button onions	1½ lb
140 g	raisins	5 oz
600 ml	dry white wine	1 pint
100 ml	olive oil	3 fl oz
100 ml	vinegar	3 fl oz
two 15 ml spoons	tomato puree	2 tablesp
one	large clove of garlic	one
one	bouquet garni (page 216)	one
one	pinch of cayenne pepper	one
	salt, pepper	

Peel the onions and put them into a pan. Add all the ingredients (crush the garlic) and a little water if the liquid does not cover the onions. Bring the contents to the boil, cover the pan, and simmer it for one hour. Check the seasoning.

Serve hot with French bread as a first course or as an accompaniment to a grill or roast. Any left-over sauce makes a good base for a soup.

Country pâté

A simple pâté, easily made, must be in every cook's repertoire. If the butcher minces the meat for you it's quicker still.

225 g	pig's liver	½ lb
225 g	lean belly of pork	½ lb
one	clove of garlic	one
100 ml	dry sherry	3 fl oz
	salt, pepper	
110 g	unsmoked streaky bacon	¼ lb

Coarsely mince the liver and pork. Mix the meat thoroughly with the crushed garlic, sherry, salt and pepper.

Remove the rind from the bacon and flatten each rasher with the back of a knife. Line a small terrine or loaf tin with the rashers, allowing them to hang over the sides of the dish, and spoon in the mixture. Fold the bacon over the top. Leave the pâté for an hour before baking it, uncovered, in a moderately slow oven (160°C, 325°F, mark 3) for one hour. Cool completely before refrigerating overnight.

Chicken liver pâté

700 g	chicken livers	1½ lb
one	large onion	one
25 g	butter	1 oz
150 ml	single cream	¼ pint
25 ml	brandy	1 fl oz
25 ml	dry sherry	1 fl oz
	salt, pepper	

Lightly fry the livers with the chopped onion in the butter. Mash the fried mixture with a fork and then liquidise it with the remaining ingredients until they are very smooth. (If you have a food processor you will not need to mash the livers first.)

Put the mixture in a small terrine and cook it, covered, in a bain-marie (page 216) in a moderately slow oven (160°C, 325°F, mark 3) for one hour. Cool the pâté and refrigerate it overnight.

Pâté en croûte

Anything wrapped in pastry seems to have a special appeal and even a pâté can be thus enhanced.

450 g	pig's liver	1 lb
one	small onion	one
one	clove of garlic	one
450 g	pork sausage-meat	1 lb
one 15 ml spoon	chopped parsley	1 tablesp
two	eggs	two
one half 5 ml spoon	mixed spice	½ teasp
	salt, pepper	
100 ml	port	3 fl oz
four	rashers of streaky bacon	four
225 g	puff pastry (page 211)	½ lb

Coarsely mince the liver, onion and garlic. Mix this with the sausage-meat, parsley, one egg, spice, salt and pepper. (Hands are best as the sausage-meat is rather sticky.) Stir in the port, and leave the mixture for one hour.

Remove the rind from the bacon and flatten each rasher with the back of a knife. Line a small loaf tin and pack the mixture in firmly. Cover the tin with foil and bake it in a moderate oven (160°C, 325°F, mark 3) for 1½ hours. Leave the pâté to cool completely before wrapping it in the pastry.

Roll the pastry out to an oblong. Remove the bacon rashers from the pâté before placing it on the pastry, upside down. Wrap the pastry round the pâté and seal the edges very well with water. Cut an air-vent, and decorate the top with trimmings before glazing it with the remaining beaten egg. Place the wrapped pâté on a dampened baking-sheet and cook it in a hot oven (200°C, 400°F, mark 6) for 30 minutes.

Leave the pâté to cool. Serve it in thick slices.

Terrine with lager

225 g	lean pork	½ lb
225 g	belly of pork	½ lb
225 g	lean pie veal	½ lb
150 ml	lager	¼ pint
six	juniper berries	six
one	clove of garlic	one
one 5 ml spoon	fresh thyme	1 teasp
	(or half quantity dried)	
one 5 ml spoon	fresh marjoram	1 teasp
	(or half quantity dried)	
	salt, pepper	

Coarsely mince the pork, belly of pork and veal, and mix them thoroughly with the remaining ingredients (crush the garlic). Leave the mixture for one hour. Pack it into a terrine, cover, and cook it in a moderately slow oven (160°C, 325°F, mark 3) for 1¼ hours. Compress the terrine under weights and leave it to cool before refrigerating it overnight.

Spanish country pâté

six	rashers of streaky bacon	six
110 g	chicken livers	¼ lb
225 g	pig's liver	½ lb
110 g	lean pie veal	¼ lb
225 g	belly of pork	½ lb
175 g	unsmoked fat bacon	6 oz
one	pinch of ground mace	one
four 5 ml spoons	fresh mixed herbs	4 teasp
	(or half quantity dried)	
two 15 ml spoons	dry sherry	2 tablesp
two 15 ml spoons	brandy	2 tablesp
two	cloves of garlic	two
	salt, pepper	

Remove the rind from the streaky bacon and flatten each rasher with the back of a knife. Line a loaf tin with the prepared bacon.

Coarsely mince together the livers, veal, belly of pork and fat bacon. Add the mace, herbs, sherry, brandy, crushed garlic, salt and pepper. Mix very well together. Pack the mixture into the lined tin. Cover the tin with foil and cook it in a bain-marie (page 216) in a slow oven (150°C, 300°F, mark 2) for two hours. Cool the pâté and refrigerate it overnight. You could press some stuffed olives into the pâté before cooking.

Pâté du chef

Since *you* are the chef, this recipe will be aptly titled, but was in fact given to me by a friendly professional.

225 g	belly of pork	½ lb
225 g	lean pie veal	½ lb
one	clove of garlic	one
one	medium-sized onion	one
two 5 ml spoons	fresh mixed herbs (or half quantity dried)	2 teasp
one	bay leaf	one
150 ml	dry white wine	¼ pint
one 15 ml spoon	brandy	1 tablesp
	salt, pepper	
450 g	back fat	1 lb
one	duck's liver (optional)	one

Coarsely mince the pork, veal, garlic and onion. Put the mixture into a bowl with the herbs. Pour over the wine and brandy and season the mixture well. Leave it to mature overnight.

Cut six strips ½-cm (¼-inch) thick from the back fat. Slice the rest very finely. In a terrine put a layer of the minced mixture, then three strips of fat, then a further layer of minced mixture. Place the whole liver in the centre. Lay the remaining strips of fat on top and cover these with the rest of the minced mixture. Cover the top layer with the remaining finely-sliced back fat. Sprinkle some more herbs over the top if you wish.

Cover the pâté and cook it in a bain-marie (page 216) in a hot oven (200°C, 400°F, mark 6) for one hour. Compress the pâté under weights and leave it to cool before refrigerating it overnight. If no duck's liver is available, you can substitute a few chicken livers, marinated in brandy.

Curried prawns

It is always useful to have a few quickly-made light meals to produce at the drop of an invitation. Frozen prawns can be quickly defrosted and made into this excellent dish.

one	*small onion*	*one*
50 g	*butter*	*2 oz*
one 15 ml spoon	*flour*	*1 tablesp*
one 15 ml spoon	*curry powder*	*1 tablesp*
five 15 ml spoons	*dry sherry*	*5 tablesp*
350 g	*peeled prawns*	*¾ lb*
	salt, pepper	
two	*egg yolks*	*two*
three 15 ml spoons	*single cream*	*3 tablesp*

Soften the finely-chopped onion in the butter. Stir in the flour and curry powder and cook the mixture for one minute. Slowly add the sherry, stirring to make a smooth sauce. Add the prawns, salt and pepper and stir well. Cover the pan and cook over a gentle heat for ten minutes. Beat the egg yolks with the cream and add the hot mixture, very slowly. Return it to the pan and warm it through over a gentle heat for a minute but do not let it boil.

Serve this with rice or in vol-au-vent cases.

Smoked mackerel pâté

Fish pâté makes a light first course before heavier things to come, or is an attractive element of a cold buffet.

225 g	*smoked mackerel*	*½ lb*
four 15 ml spoons	*dry cider*	*4 tablesp*
two 15 ml spoons	*single cream*	*2 tablesp*
	salt, pepper	
50 g	*melted butter*	*2 oz*

Remove the skin and bones from the mackerel and flake the flesh. Liquidise or process the fish with all the other ingredients until it is smooth. Put the pâté into a serving-dish or individual dishes. Refrigerate until firm, overnight if possible.

Tuna pâté

425 g	tinned tuna	15 oz
110 g	butter	1/4 lb
50 ml	olive oil	2 fl oz
one	lemon	one
one	small onion	one
two 15 ml spoons	aquavit	2 tablesp
one	hard-boiled egg	one

Drain the oil from the tuna and then combine all the ingredients (juice of the lemon only) except the egg in a liquidiser or food processor until the mixture is smooth (a liquidiser will probably require two batches).

Turn the pâté into a shallow serving dish or individual pots and refrigerate until it is firm (overnight if possible). Decorate with slices of hard-boiled egg.

You could make an aspic (I use a packet) adding a little aquavit to the liquid. Spoon it over the pâté when it is beginning to set.

Replace the aquavit with kümmel or vodka, if you wish.

Beer and cheese spread

This quickly-made spread will appeal to beer drinkers. It is good as an appetizer or part of a cheese table for a cheese and wine (or beer?) party.

175 ml	light ale	6 fl oz
110 g	cottage cheese	1/4 lb
110 g	Cheddar cheese	1/4 lb
one	large pickled cucumber	one

Liquidise all the ingredients until they are smooth. Serve on crackers or as a dip.

For a stronger version, use up ends of old cheese (mild, tangy, blue, what you will . . .), add dry mustard or Worcestershire sauce if you wish, and store the spread in the refrigerator for several days to mature.

Swiss cheese pudding

This savoury bread-and-butter pudding is my idea of a perfect Sunday supper dish.

	butter	
twelve	slices of white bread	twelve
225 g	grated Gruyère	1/2 lb
three	eggs	three
300 ml	dry white wine	1/2 pint
150 ml	chicken stock (page 215)	1/4 pint
150 ml	single cream	1/4 pint
	salt, pepper	

Butter an oven-proof dish and put half the bread (with the crusts removed) in the dish. Scatter the grated cheese over the bread. Butter the rest of the bread and place it on top of the cheese. Mix the eggs with the wine, stock, cream and seasonings, and pour the liquid over the bread. Leave it to soak for half an hour. Cook it in a moderate oven (180°C, 350°F, mark 4) for 45 minutes.

Cheese fondue

The only requisites for this Swiss dish are a group of hungry people and a fondue set.

one	clove of garlic	one
600 ml	dry white wine	1 pint
450 g	Cheddar, grated	1 lb
450 g	Gruyère, grated	1 lb
two 15 ml spoons	cornflour	2 tablesp
two 15 ml spoons	kirsch	2 tablesp
	grated nutmeg	
	pepper	
	bread cut into 1.5-cm (3/4-inch) cubes	

Rub a flame-proof dish or pan with the cut garlic. Pour the wine into the pan and add a third of the grated cheese. Put the pan on the spirit stove over moderate heat. Stir the mixture and as the cheese begins to melt, gradually add the rest of the cheese. Mix the cornflour with the kirsch and when all the cheese has melted, stir in the cornflour mixture. Add a little grated nutmeg and some freshly-ground pepper. When the mixture begins to boil, reduce the heat and keep the fondue cooking gently.

Arm your guests with long fondue forks with which they can spear pieces of bread to dip into the melted cheese. I always find that though this is most delicious, it is very filling. A few slices of apple to dip into the fondue make a welcome change from all the bread.

Meurette d'oeufs

It may seem a little extravagant to use such a lot of wine to cook eggs, but this makes a very substantial lunch or supper dish. Try the recipe with rosé wine for a change, for a gentler colour and taste.

four–six	*slices of white bread*	*four–six*
	oil	
110 g	*button mushrooms*	*¼ lb*
	butter	
300 ml	*red wine*	*½ pint*
one	*bouquet garni (page 216)*	*one*
one	*clove of garlic*	*one*
four–six	*eggs*	*four–six*
one 15 ml spoon	*flour*	*1 tablesp*
	salt, pepper	

Remove the crusts from the bread and fry it in the oil until it is golden brown. Drain the slices well and keep them warm. Toss the sliced mushrooms in a little butter to colour them. Drain them and keep them warm.

Put the wine into a frying-pan together with the bouquet garni and the crushed garlic. Bring the wine quickly to the boil and then reduce it to simmering-point. Poach the eggs in the wine (crack them first into a cup, one at a time, and slip them into the pan; poach only as many as the pan will conveniently hold). Drain the eggs and keep them warm while you poach the remainder.

Mix the flour with a little cold water and add it to the wine. Season well and cook until the sauce is smooth, stirring all the time. You may need to add a little more wine, and you could add some water at this stage. Add the reserved mushrooms to the sauce and simmer for a few minutes while you are putting the eggs on the fried bread. Spoon the sauce over the eggs and serve them immediately.

Oeufs Céline

The restaurant in Paris in which I saw this unusual dish no doubt used real caviar. Since it is rather a light-hearted start to a meal, I would use the more mundane, but perfectly acceptable, lumpfish roe.

four–six	*large fresh eggs*	*four–six*
four–six 5 ml spoons	*lumpfish roe*	*4–6 teasp*
three 15 ml spoons	*vodka*	*3 tablesp*

Lightly boil the eggs – three minutes should be right. Remove them from the water and quickly cut off the tops, placing the eggs in pottery or metal eggcups. Stand the eggcups in a shallow, flame-proof dish. Put a spoonful of lumpfish roe on each egg.

Warm the vodka in a soup ladle, ignite it and pour it over the eggs. Serve while still flaming (if possible!), with hot French bread or crispbread. If you want to make a more substantial course of this, serve two eggs per person.

Uova al marsala

Eggs often tend to be relegated to the breakfast menu, but this is decidedly for sophisticated suppers.

six–nine	*eggs*	*six–nine*
110 g	*sliced ham*	*¼ lb*
half	*green pepper*	*half*
25 g	*butter*	*1 oz*
110 g	*button mushrooms*	*¼ lb*
150 ml	*single cream*	*¼ pint*
100 ml	*marsala*	*3 fl oz*
	pepper	

Hard-boil the eggs. Cut the ham and the green pepper into thin strips. Toss them in melted butter for a few minutes. Add the sliced mushrooms and cook them, stirring from time to time, until they are soft. Stir in the cream and marsala and warm the sauce through. Season with freshly-ground pepper. Put the peeled and halved eggs in a shallow dish and spoon the sauce over them. Serve with fried bread croûtons or hot French bread.

Courgettes in red wine

Don't feel guilty serving a plain grill or roast when you have these delicious courgettes to accompany it. On the other hand, you could make an excellent first course by serving them on fried bread.

700 g	courgettes	1½ lb
	olive oil and butter	
one	Spanish onion	one
150 ml	red wine	¼ pint
	salt, pepper	
two 15 ml spoons	lemon juice	2 tablesp
	chopped parsley	

Cut the unpeeled courgettes into 1-cm (½-inch) slices. Toss them in a sauté-pan in oil and butter over a low heat, together with the finely-chopped onion. Stir the mixture from time to time. Add the wine and seasoning and simmer for five minutes. Sprinkle the courgettes with the lemon juice, one 5-ml (tea) spoon of olive oil and the parsley, and serve hot.

Fettuccine con funghi freschi

Although noodles are strictly speaking the pasta you need for this, the tasty mushrooms which accompany it are just as good on spaghetti or whatever you have handy.

one	large clove of garlic	one
two 15 ml spoons	olive oil	2 tablesp
450 g	button mushrooms	1 lb
200 ml	dry white wine	7 fl oz
two 15 ml spoons	chopped parsley	2 tablesp
450 g	noodles	1 lb
50 g	butter	2 oz
50 g	grated Parmesan	2 oz
	salt, pepper	

To make the sauce, sauté the chopped garlic in the oil. Add the sliced mushrooms to the pan. Cook them for a few minutes, lower the heat and add the wine. Cook until the wine has just evaporated. Add the chopped parsley and simmer for a further five minutes.

Boil the pasta in salted water till *al dente*. Drain it. Turn it into a large bowl and add the butter, Parmesan, salt and freshly-ground black pepper. Stir in the mushrooms and serve the fettuccine immediately on very hot plates.

Risotto alla milanese

Italians, to my mind quite rightly, make a whole course out of this delightful dish instead of using it as an adjunct to meat and two veg. Saffron is classically correct, turmeric cheaper.

one	*large onion*	*one*
75 g	*butter*	*3 oz*
450 g	*Italian rice*	*1 lb*
¼ of a 5 ml spoon	*saffron or*	*¼ teasp*
one half 5 ml spoon	*turmeric*	*½ teasp*
1 litre	*chicken stock (page 215)*	*1¾ pints*
225 ml	*dry white wine*	*8 fl oz*
75 g	*grated Parmesan*	*3 oz*
	salt, pepper	

Fry the finely-chopped onion in the butter in a large, heavy pan, until it is golden. Add the rice and turmeric and stir until the butter is absorbed (if you are using saffron, add it along with the stock). Add the stock and wine. Cook, uncovered, over a gentle heat, stirring from time to time. When the rice is almost cooked, add the remaining butter and a spoonful of the cheese. Season the rice to taste. Serve the remaining Parmesan separately.

If you are serving the risotto as a separate course, add sautéed sliced mushrooms to it if you wish.

Fish

Fish has become something of a luxury in recent years and that highlights the question of whether a lot of fancy dressing up is really necessary, given good, fresh fish. Therein, of course, lies the rub . . . first catch your fresh fish. As most of us aren't able to do that, the next problem is to find a fishmonger – and sadly they are a species on their way to extinction.

Even if you do have a reliable fishmonger you may still want to prepare your fish with some adornment. A sauce, simple but exquisite, is the perfect accompaniment to good fish. If you haven't tried beurre blanc you have a real treat in store.

Frozen fish is fairly widely available, and while the amateur fisherman might turn his nose up at the very thought of such an aberration, many people prefer it to much of the so-called fresh fish which is obtainable. It is anyway a very useful standby in the freezer as it defrosts very quickly.

For some of us perhaps the greatest virtue of fish is that it is so low in calories, and even with the addition of a little dry white wine you can satisfy your most calorie-conscious friends.

Many of these dishes would make ideal first courses, in which case you should reduce the quantities by about half.

Poisson à la normande

Use any white fish for this recipe: plaice, sole, haddock, or whatever the fishmonger is offering.

1 litre	mussels	1 quart
225 g	prawns in shell	½ lb
300 ml	dry white wine	½ pint
300 ml	water	½ pint
one	small onion	one
one	small carrot	one
	parsley stalks	
one	lemon	one
	salt, pepper	
1 kg	fillets of white fish	2 lb
	butter	
225 g	button mushrooms	½ lb
two 15 ml spoons	flour	2 tablesp
one	egg yolk	one

Scrub the mussels well and remove any barnacles and beards. Discard any that are open. Put them into a large pan with two cupsful of water and cook them, covered, over a high heat, shaking the pan frequently until they have opened. Discard any which do not open. Remove the mussels from the shells and reserve them. In a saucepan combine the prawn shells with the wine, water, finely-chopped onion and carrot, the parsley stalks, the sliced lemon, salt and pepper. Bring the mixture to the boil, reduce the heat, and simmer it for ten minutes. Strain the liquid into a shallow, flame-proof dish.

Lay the fillets in the dish and poach them gently, covered, for ten minutes. Carefully remove the fish from the liquid and put it into a lightly-buttered oven-proof dish. Season it well, dot it with butter and put the sliced mushrooms on top. Cover the dish and cook it in a moderate oven (180°C, 350°F, mark 4) for ten minutes. Strain the cooking liquid into a saucepan.

Make a beurre manié (page 216) with two 15 ml (table) spoons butter and the flour and add it to the liquid, a little at a time, over a medium heat, beating after each addition, until you have a smooth, fairly thick sauce. Beat the egg yolk and slowly add the sauce, a drop at a time, beating constantly. Return the sauce to the pan, add a squeeze of lemon juice, the reserved mussels and prawns, and salt and pepper. Warm everything through over a very gentle heat.

Remove the fish from the oven, spoon over the sauce and serve the dish immediately.

Poisson braisé à la dieppoise

	butter	
two	shallots	two
four–six	individual fish or fillets (red mullet, turbot, sole, plaice)	four–six
	salt, pepper	
200 ml	dry white wine	7 fl oz
six 15 ml spoons	double cream	6 tablesp
110 g	cooked, shelled mussels, and/or shrimps or prawns	1/4 lb

Butter a shallow flame-proof dish and sprinkle it with the finely-chopped shallots. Place the fish in the dish, season it well and pour on the wine. Cover the dish with buttered paper or foil and cook it in a moderate oven (180°C, 350°F, mark 4) for 30 minutes, basting it occasionally.

When the fish is ready, remove it from the dish and keep it warm. Add the cream to the cooking liquid and bring it gently to the boil. Add the shellfish and warm them through. Pour the sauce over the fish and serve it immediately with pureed potatoes, perhaps, or French bread and a green salad.

Sole with sherry

six	small soles	six
110 g	mushrooms	1/4 lb
50 g	butter	2 oz
	salt, pepper	
150 ml	dry sherry	1/4 pint
four 15 ml spoons	double cream	4 tablesp

Ask the fishmonger to fillet each sole into two fillets. Slice the mushrooms and scatter them over the fish. Place dots of butter on the fish, season them well and fold the fillets in half. Place them in a shallow, oven-proof dish. Add the sherry, cover, and cook the fish in a moderate oven (180°C, 350°F, mark 4) for 25 minutes. Remove the dish from the oven, strain off the juices into a saucepan and keep the fish warm. Add the cream to the liquid and cook it over a high heat to reduce and thicken it. Pour the sauce over the fish and serve it immediately.

Catalan fish salad

We don't seem to think of eating fresh fish cold very much but this is an unusual and rather refreshing salad with mussels and prawns. It makes an excellent first course or a main dish, served with hot bread or a potato salad, hot or cold.

1 kg	mussels	2 lb
175 ml	dry white wine	6 fl oz
one	crisp lettuce	one
two	sticks of celery	two
one	red pepper	one
one	green pepper	one
one 15 ml spoon	chopped mint	1 tablesp
two 15 ml spoons	chopped parsley	2 tablesp
175 g	peeled prawns	6 oz
110 g	cooked peas	4 oz
five 15 ml spoons	olive oil	5 tablesp
two 15 ml spoons	wine vinegar	2 tablesp
	salt, pepper	

Scrub the mussels thoroughly under cold running water, scraping them with a sharp knife to remove any barnacles and beards. Throw away any mussels which have already opened. Put them in a large pan with the wine. Cover the pan and bring them to the boil. Simmer them until they have opened. Drain them, reserving the liquid. Discard any which do not open. Remove the mussels from the shells and reserve them.

Shred the lettuce and put it into a large salad bowl with the chopped celery and peppers (with the seeds removed), the mint and the parsley. Add first the peeled prawns and mussels to the salad bowl, then the cooked peas. Make a dressing with the oil and vinegar. If you like, you can add a little of the liquid in which the mussels were cooked. Season the salad well and toss it before serving.

Remember that if you are buying the prawns in their shells you will need enough to yield 175 g/6 oz, so buy at least 280 g/10 oz. Add prawns and mussels if you wish.

The liquid from the mussels can be used as the base of a fish stock and if you have the prawn shells you can add them to the mussel liquid, with a little more wine, some water, parsley stalks and a few peppercorns. Cook for about ten minutes and then strain the stock, leave it to cool, and freeze it for use in a fish soup (for example, page 25).

Fisherman's casserole

Any white fish will do for this tasty dish and you can add or subtract the other fishy ingredients.

300 ml	fish stock (page 215)	½ pint
300 ml	dry white wine	½ pint
700 g	white fish fillets	1½ lb
two	scallops (optional)	two
one	medium-sized onion	one
50 g	butter	2 oz
50 g	flour	2 oz
one	pinch of cayenne pepper	one
two	large tomatoes	two
	salt, pepper	
110 g	peeled prawns	¼ lb
three 15 ml spoons	single cream	3 tablesp

Heat the stock and wine in a shallow pan and add the fish fillets and scallops, cut into large pieces. Poach the fish for five minutes. Soften the chopped onion in the melted butter. Add the flour and stir it in off the heat to make a smooth paste. Very slowly add the liquid from the fish, stirring it until it is smooth. Return the pan to the heat and cook the sauce gently until it has thickened. Add the fish, cayenne pepper and tomatoes (skinned, seeded and cut into strips) and season everything well with salt and pepper. Add the prawns and warm them through. Stir in the cream and serve the dish immediately.

You could make a more substantial dish by topping the fish with some mashed potatoes. Or use half the quantity as a vol-au-vent filling for a first course.

Sole bourguignonne

The old rule about not serving red wine with fish is broken here to very interesting effect.

	butter	
	butter	
twelve	small fillets of sole	twelve
three	shallots	three
225 g	button mushrooms	½ lb
	salt, pepper	
200 ml	red wine	7 fl oz
	flour	

Lightly butter a shallow oven-proof dish. Lay the fillets of sole in the dish and scatter the finely-chopped shallots and sliced mushrooms around the fish. Season it well. Add the wine, cover, and cook the fish in a moderate oven (180°C, 350°F, mark 4) for 25 minutes.

Pour off the liquid and keep the fish warm while you make the sauce. Heat the liquid and thicken it by adding beurre manié (page 216) a little at a time until the desired thickness is obtained. Pour the sauce over the sole and serve it immediately with croûtons or pureed potatoes.

Sole in cider

six	small soles	six
	butter	
two	shallots	two
	chopped parsley	
	salt, pepper	
150 ml	dry cider	¼ pint
three 15 ml spoons	single cream	3 tablesp

Clean the soles and remove the heads. Lay them in a buttered, shallow oven-proof dish with the finely-chopped shallots and the chopped parsley. Season the fish well. Pour on the cider and cook the fish, covered, in a moderately slow oven (160°C, 325°F, mark 3) for 25 minutes. Add the cream and warm it through gently.

Serve with new or pureed potatoes.

Fish with melon

This is an Israeli version of the classic sole Véronique, with melon replacing the grapes.

one	medium-sized onion	one
	butter	
twelve	small fillets of sole, lemon sole or plaice	twelve
	salt, pepper	
200 ml	dry white wine	7 fl oz
25 g	butter	1 oz
25 g	flour	1 oz
one	honeydew melon	one
150 ml	single cream	¼ pint

Place the finely-chopped onion on the bottom of a buttered oven-proof dish. Season the fish and roll up each fillet. Place the fish in the dish. Pour on the wine, cover the dish, and cook it in a moderate oven (180°C, 350°F, mark 4) for 20 minutes.

While the fish is cooking, make a roux (page 217) with the butter and flour. When the fish is ready, strain off the cooking-liquid onto the roux. Keep the fish warm. Stir the sauce over a gentle heat until it is smooth and thick. Add the melon, cut into cubes or balls, and the cream. Warm everything through. Spoon the sauce over the fish and serve it with new or pureed potatoes.

Halibut with cream sauce

1 kg	halibut steaks	2 lb
	butter	
	salt, pepper	
300 ml	dry white wine	½ pint
three	egg yolks	three
one 5 ml spoon	cornflour	1 teasp
225 ml	single cream	8 fl oz
one 15 ml spoon	capers	1 tablesp

Put the fish in a buttered, shallow flame-proof dish, and season it well. Pour on the wine, cover the dish, and simmer the contents for ten minutes, or until the fish is cooked.

Carefully lift the fish onto a serving-dish and keep it warm while you make the sauce. Reduce the liquid to half by boiling. Mix the egg yolks with the cornflour and cream and drip the hot liquid into this mixture, very slowly, stirring constantly. Return the sauce to the pan and warm it through over a low heat until it has thickened but not boiled. Add the capers and pour the sauce over the fish.

Halibut with vermouth

The sauce is what makes this interesting, so it would taste just as good with a less expensive fish like haddock, cod, monk-fish or huss. Use either dry or sweet vermouth.

1 kg	*halibut steaks*	*2 lb*
100 ml	*white vermouth*	*3 fl oz*
one	*orange*	*one*
25 g	*butter*	*1 oz*
	salt, pepper	
one	*orange*	*one*
	watercress	

Marinate the halibut in the vermouth for half an hour or more. Place the fish and its marinade in a shallow baking-dish and add the juice of the orange and a little grated rind. Dot with the butter and season well. Cover the fish with foil and cook it in a moderate oven (180°C, 350°F, mark 4) for 35 minutes. If you prefer a thicker sauce, remove the fish and reduce the liquid a little.

Garnish with thin slices of orange and the watercress.

Moules marinière

I couldn't decide how to classify this recipe – as a soup, an hors d'oeuvre or here with the fish. It could quite comfortably fit into any of these categories. You could cut down on the liquid and make it less soupy, or on the quantity and make it more of an hors d'oeuvre.

3 litres	*mussels*	*2½ quarts*
two	*shallots*	*two*
one	*bouquet garni (page 216)*	*one*
75 g	*butter*	*3 oz*
600 ml	*dry white wine*	*1 pint*
50 g	*flour*	*2 oz*
three 15 ml spoons	*chopped parsley*	*3 tablesp*

Scrub the mussels well and remove any barnacles and beards. Discard any that are open. Put them into a large pan with the chopped shallots, the bouquet garni, one third of the butter and the wine. Cover the pan and shake it over a high heat until they have opened. Discard any that do not open.

Put the mussels into a large tureen. Strain the liquid through a sieve lined with kitchen paper or muslin into a clean pan, and bring it to the boil. Add some beurre manié (page 216) made with the rest of the butter and the flour and whisk it into the liquid to make a smooth sauce. Pour the sauce over the mussels, sprinkle them with the chopped parsley and serve immediately.

If you prefer an unthickened broth, leave out the beurre manié.

Mussels in sherry

3 litres	mussels	2½ quarts
150 ml	dry white wine	¼ pint
150 ml	water	¼ pint
two	cloves of garlic	two
four 15 ml spoons	chopped parsley	4 tablesp
100 ml	olive oil	3 fl oz
one	medium-sized onion	one
one 15 ml spoon	flour	1 tablesp
125 ml	dry sherry	4 fl oz

Scrub the mussels well and remove any barnacles and beards. Discard any that are open. Put them into a large pan with the wine and water. Cover the pan and shake it over a high heat until the mussels have opened. Discard any that do not open. Remove the mussels from the shells and reserve them. Strain the liquid through a sieve lined with kitchen paper or muslin and reserve it.

Crush the garlic and mix it with the parsley and half the oil. Fry the finely-chopped onion in the remaining oil until it is soft. Remove the pan from the heat and stir in the flour. Add 150 ml (¼ pint) of the reserved liquid. Stir it in and return the pan to the heat. Continue stirring the sauce until it is smooth. Add the mussels and the garlic-and-parsley mixture. Simmer the sauce for five minutes. Add the sherry and warm it through.

Serve the mussels in individual pots with hot garlic bread.

Cod with sherry

1 kg	cod fillets	2 lb
	salt, pepper	
50 ml	olive oil	2 fl oz
75 ml	dry sherry	3 fl oz
50 g	flaked almonds	2 oz

Place the fish in a shallow oven-proof dish and season it well. Pour on the oil and sherry. Scatter the almonds over the fish. Cover the dish and cook it in a moderate oven (190°C, 375°F, mark 5) for 20 minutes.

Salmon trout in white wine

one	small salmon trout (about 1.25 kg/2½ lb)	one
	salt, pepper	
350 g	mushrooms	¾ lb
350 ml	dry white wine	12 fl oz
one	lemon	one
50 g	butter	2 oz
two 15 ml spoons	duxelles (page 217)	2 tablesp
225 g	tomatoes	½ lb

Clean the fish, discarding the head. Season well and place it in an oven-proof dish. Surround the fish with the sliced mushrooms. Pour over the wine and the juice of the lemon. Dot small pieces of butter over the fish.

Cover the dish and cook it in a moderate oven (180°C, 350°F, mark 4) for 30 minutes. Pour off the juices into a pan and add the duxelles and the tomatoes, peeled, seeded and cut into strips. Warm the sauce through and pour it over the fish.

Creamed crab

Frozen crab (both white and brown meat) is perfectly suitable for this recipe, which would make a first course served alone or a main course with rice.

25 g	butter	1 oz
25 g	flour	1 oz
350 ml	milk	12 fl oz
quarter 5 ml spoon	grated nutmeg	¼ teasp
	salt, pepper	
two	hard-boiled egg yolks	two
225 g	button mushrooms	½ lb
one 15 ml spoon	butter	1 tablesp
225 g	cooked crab-meat	½ lb
50 ml	marsala	2 fl oz

Make a béchamel (page 182) with the 25 g (1 oz) butter, flour and milk. Add the nutmeg, salt and pepper, and fold in the mashed egg yolks. Cook the sliced mushrooms in the remaining butter, just enough to colour them. Flake the crab-meat and add it to the sauce, along with the mushrooms. Stir in the marsala. Adjust the seasoning. Serve either with rice, as a filling for vol-au-vents, with a puff pastry topping as a pie, in individual ramekins or on croûtons.

Coquilles St Jacques au cidre

12–18 (or 450–700 g)	*scallops*	*12–18 (1–1½ lb)*
three	*shallots*	*three*
50 g	*butter*	*2 oz*
½ litre	*dry cider*	*17 fl oz*
	salt, pepper	
one 15 ml spoon	*cornflour*	*1 teasp*
100 ml	*double cream*	*3 fl oz*
100 ml	*single cream*	*3 fl oz*
one	*squeeze of lemon*	*one*

Wash the scallops and remove any discoloured parts. Pat them dry and slice them.

Soften the finely-chopped shallots in the melted butter in a shallow pan. Add the cider, the scallops, salt and pepper. Bring the liquid to the boil, reduce the heat, and allow it to simmer for ten minutes. Remove the scallops and keep them warm.

Reduce the cooking liquid by half by boiling. Mix the cornflour with the cream and add it to the pan. Stir the sauce as it thickens and simmer it for three minutes. Return the scallops to the sauce and add a squeeze of lemon. Serve with rice.

Mackerel in white wine

I first had mackerel in white wine in a Paris restaurant where it was served in the tin –
the ultimate in haute cuisine you might think. But it was so delicious I have been trying
to copy it ever since, coming to the sad conclusion that this is one case where the tinned
product is better than the home-made one. Well, different, anyway. It is an ideal
slimmer's recipe. Try the recipe with herring too.

three	*mackerel (about 450 g/1 lb each)*	*three*
one	*medium-sized onion*	*one*
four	*slices of lemon*	*four*
one and a half 15 ml spoons	*pickling spice*	*1½ tablesp*
two	*bay leaves*	*two*
	salt, pepper	
350 ml	*dry white wine*	*12 fl oz*
150 ml	*water*	*¼ pint*

Clean the fish and remove the heads. Place them in a shallow fire-proof dish or frying-
pan. Lay the thinly-sliced onion on the fish, along with the lemon slices. Sprinkle over
the spice, the crumbled bay leaves and salt and pepper. Add the wine and water. Cover
the fish and cook it over a gentle heat for 30 minutes, turning the fish halfway through
the cooking. The liquid should barely simmer. The fish is ready when it comes away
from the backbone if pressed gently.

Remove the pan from the heat and leave the fish to cool. Skin it and refrigerate it, if
possible overnight, since it is best eaten really cold.

To serve, divide the fish into fillets, spoon over the sauce, and decorate it with the onion
and lemon slices.

For a first course, use half the amount of fish.

Meat

There are many people who prefer their meat plain and simple – the roast beef of old England, a grilled lamb chop or a veal cutlet – all *au naturel*. Undoubtedly there is much to be said for this point of view, although it would soon put cookery-book writers out of business. I think it is as difficult to produce a perfectly-cooked joint of meat or steak as it is to make an elaborate casserole, but for a dinner party I find it more relaxing to have a previously-prepared dish ready and waiting than to have to worry about the meat being overcooked if the guests happen to be rather late.

For the adventurous cook, I hope the following recipes will provide some variety not only in meals for visitors, but for family dinners too.

Beef

Unlike a rose, which is a rose, is a rose, a daube is not only a daube, is a daube, but also a casserole, stew, estouffade (or estouffat); it even has several other names. Pedants will no doubt tell me that there are subtle differences in these various dishes, but (coming back to the rose) a stew by any other name will taste as good. Beef, perhaps more than any other meat, lends itself to cooking with wine and beer. Wine especially helps to break down tough fibres, and it is for this reason that many recipes suggest marinating the meat for several days. The habit of using wine in this way has long been prevalent in regions of France noted for their rather tough meat.

I have not included recipes for steak as such, but if you are planning a grilled meat dish and want to jazz it up, try a sauce from the sauce section (page 179). It will salve your conscience to feel that you are making some effort, and even the juiciest of steaks can be enhanced by a good sauce.

Boeuf Avignon

There seem to be both a red-wine and a white-wine version of this recipe, which makes it versatile.

2 kg	topside of beef	4 lb
three 15 ml spoons	olive oil	3 tablesp
600 ml	red or dry white wine	1 pint
two	cloves of garlic	two
one	lemon	one
one	bay leaf	one
one	medium-sized onion	one
	mixed herbs (fresh or dried)	
	pepper	
three	rashers of streaky bacon	three
450 g	button onions	1 lb
225 g	mushrooms	½ lb
four	large tomatoes	four
300 ml	beef stock (page 214)	½ pint

Marinate the meat (in one piece) overnight in the oil, wine, crushed garlic, lemon juice, bay leaf, sliced onion, finely-chopped fresh herbs (or dried mixed herbs) and pepper.

Chop the bacon and place it in a casserole large enough to hold the beef. Put the meat on top and add the peeled button onions, sliced mushrooms and peeled tomatoes. Pour over the marinade and stock. Cover the casserole with foil and its lid. Cook in a slow oven (150°C, 300°F, mark 2) for three hours. Cook for a further two hours on the following day if possible. If necessary, add more liquid in the same proportion of stock to wine.

Sauerbraten

Charlemagne is believed to have invented Sauerbraten, which is one of Germany's most popular dishes. Though wine is not always used in it, this version requires wine in both the marinade and the accompanying sauce.

2 kg	*rump or topside of beef*	*4 lb*
600 ml	*red wine*	*1 pint*
150 ml	*red wine vinegar*	*1/4 pint*
one 5 ml spoon	*salt*	*1 teasp*
one 5 ml spoon	*peppercorns*	*1 teasp*
half 5 ml spoon	*dried thyme*	*1/2 teasp*
half 5 ml spoon	*ground mace*	*1/2 teasp*
half 5 ml spoon	*ground allspice*	*1/2 teasp*
one 5 ml spoon	*dry mustard*	*1 teasp*
three	*bay leaves*	*three*
ten	*cloves*	*ten*
225 g	*onions*	*1/2 lb*
three	*sticks of celery*	*three*
	flour	
	oil	
six	*gingersnaps*	*six*
150 ml	*sour cream*	*1/4 pint*
50 ml	*dry madeira*	*2 fl oz*

Put the beef into an earthenware pot with the wine, vinegar, seasonings, and chopped onions and celery. Cover the pot and leave the meat to marinate for two to four days, turning it several times each day. The pot can be left in a cool place; it need not be refrigerated.

When you wish to cook the meat, remove it from the pot and pat it dry with kitchen paper. Pass it through the flour and brown it well on all sides in the hot oil. Strain the marinade over the meat. Cover the pot and simmer it for three hours, or cook it in a slow oven (150°C, 300°F, mark 2).

Remove the meat from the casserole and stir into the juices the crushed biscuits, the sour cream and the madeira. Warm the sauce through gently and serve it with the sliced meat.

Red cabbage is a traditional accompaniment to Sauerbraten.

Beef olives

Whether you call them beef olives, rolls, paupiettes or birds, they are always thin slices of beef rolled round a stuffing of other meats, and cooked gently in wine.

1 kg	beef (see below)	2 lb
450 g	minced veal	1 lb
one	small onion	one
one 15 ml spoon	chopped parsley	1 tablesp
one	pinch of grated nutmeg	one
	salt, pepper	
	oil	
one	large onion	one
one	large carrot	one
one 15 ml spoon	flour	1 tablesp
300 ml	beef stock	1/2 pint
300 ml	red wine	1/2 pint
one	bouquet garni (page 216)	one
225 g	button mushrooms	1/2 lb

Use either topside, top rump or 'leg of mutton' cut. Ask your butcher to cut the meat into very thin slices and flatten them well. Trim off any fat.

Make a stuffing with the veal, grated onion, parsley, nutmeg, salt and pepper. Divide the stuffing into as many spoonsful as you have slices of beef. Place a spoonful of stuffing on each slice. Roll up the beef and secure it either with a toothpick or by tying some cotton round it.

Heat a little oil in a frying-pan and brown the rolls. Transfer them to a casserole and add the sliced onion and carrot to the frying-pan. Toss them to colour them a little before putting them on top of the beef. Sprinkle the flour over the remaining oil in the frying-pan and stir it well. Slowly add the stock, stirring to make a smooth sauce. Add the wine, salt and pepper before pouring the sauce over the meat. Add the bouquet garni to the casserole, cover it, and cook it in a slow oven (150°C, 300°F, mark 2) for two hours.

Take the rolls out of the casserole and remove the toothpicks or cotton. Return the meat to the casserole, add the mushrooms (left whole if they are small) and cook for a further 30 minutes.

With this basic recipe you can make your own variations ad infinitum:

Change the meat: use pork tenderloin or veal or turkey escalopes, beaten out thin.

Change the stuffing: use sausage-meat and different spices and herbs; use pork and veal mixed, or just pork; add some sherry or madeira to the stuffing; make a mixture of breadcrumbs, onion and herbs, with an egg to bind it.

Change the sauce: use white wine instead of red; dry vermouth; half the quantity of sherry; make a Provencal sauce by adding tomatoes and olives.

Boeuf en daube

A daube is invariably made with beef – except for daube à l'avignonnaise, which uses lamb or mutton. Most districts in France have their own particular version, with local herbs and ingredients. The important point is to cook it for a very long time at a very low temperature. This version spreads the cooking over two days.

110 g	streaky bacon	1/4 lb
1.5 kg	topside of beef	3 lb
three	cloves of garlic	three
	oil or pork fat	
two	medium-sized onions	two
two 15 ml spoons	flour	2 tablesp
300 ml	beef stock (page 214)	1/2 pint
450 g	carrots	1 lb
300 ml	red wine	1/2 pint
400 g	tinned tomatoes	14 oz
one	bouquet garni (page 216)	one
	salt, pepper	
225 g	button mushrooms	8 oz

Cut the bacon into thin strips and lard the beef with it. (If you have no larding needle, make slits in the meat with a pointed knife and poke the bacon strips in.) Insert small pieces of garlic in the incisions. Brown the meat well in the hot fat. Remove it and cook the sliced onions in the fat until they are soft. Stir in the flour. Add the stock and stir until the sauce is smooth.

Return the meat to the pan; arrange the sliced carrots round it. Pour over the wine, sieve the tomatoes over the meat, and add the herbs and plenty of salt and pepper. Cover the pan and cook it in a very slow oven (140°C, 275°F, mark 1) for four hours. Add the mushrooms and cook the casserole for a further two hours the following day.

Steak and kidney pie

The addition of ale to this old favourite gives a splendid richness to the gravy.

one	large onion	one
	oil or dripping	
1 kg	stewing steak	2 lb
	seasoned flour	
300 ml	beef stock (page 214)	½ pint
300 ml	dark ale	½ pint
two 5 ml spoons	fresh mixed herbs	2 teasp
	(or half quantity dried)	
225 g	kidneys	½ lb
110 g	button mushrooms	¼ lb
225 g	puff pastry (page 211)	½ lb
one	egg	one

In a large, flame-proof casserole, soften the sliced onion in the oil. Cube the meat and pass it through the seasoned flour. Brown it in the casserole with the onion. Add the stock, ale and herbs to the casserole. Stir it well and bring the liquid to the boil. Cover the casserole and cook it in a moderately slow oven (160°C, 325°F, mark 3) for two hours. Cut the kidneys in half and remove the cores. Slice them thickly. Slice the mushrooms (or leave them whole if you prefer). Toss the kidneys and mushrooms briefly in a little oil to colour them.

Remove the casserole from the oven and turn the meat into a pie-dish just deep enough to hold it. Add the kidneys and mushrooms. Roll the pastry out to fit the top of the dish when the meat has cooled somewhat. Seal the edges well. Cut an air-vent, decorate the top with pastry trimmings, and brush with the beaten egg (or the white alone if preferred). Cook the pie in a hot oven (200°C, 400°F, mark 6) for ten minutes, and then reduce the heat to 190°C (375°F, mark 5) for 15–20 minutes.

Fillet of beef with port

While this is similar to beef Stroganoff (page 75), the flavour is sufficiently different to tempt me to include it. Ruby port would be ideal, but any port in a storm.

one	*medium-sized onion*	*one*
	butter	
700 g	*beef fillet*	*1½ lb*
	salt, pepper	
225 g	*tomatoes*	*½ lb*
225 g	*button mushrooms*	*½ lb*
150 ml	*port*	*¼ pint*
150 ml	*single cream*	*¼ pint*

Soften the finely-chopped onion in butter. Cut the beef into narrow strips, season it well, and toss it in the pan for five minutes. Remove it and keep it warm. Add the peeled, seeded and chopped tomatoes and whole mushrooms (quarter them if they are large). Add the port and check the seasoning. Cook for a further five minutes. Return the beef to the pan, add the cream, and gently bring the sauce to just below boiling-point.

A friendly butcher might be able to sell you the tail-end of a fillet at considerably less than the very expensive whole fillet. Since it has to be cut into small pieces, the ends are quite suitable.

Baeckaoffa

This is a hearty peasant dish, more for family meals than elegant dinner parties. Its strange name might provide a clue to its origins, for linguists and lovers of Alsace. Ideally the wine used should be a Sylvaner from that area.

450 g	lean stewing beef	1 lb
225 g	boned shoulder of lamb	½ lb
225 g	boned shoulder of pork	½ lb
300 ml	dry white wine	½ pint
	thyme	
one	bay leaf	one
one 15 ml spoon	chopped parsley	1 tablesp
	salt, pepper	
	butter	
four	large onions	four
four	large potatoes	four

Cut all the meat into 5-cm (2-inch) cubes, trimming off excess fat. Put it into a large bowl and pour over the wine. Add the herbs, salt and pepper. Leave the meat to marinate overnight in a cool place.

Grease a large casserole with the butter. Put a layer of sliced onions and potatoes on the bottom of the casserole. Add a layer of meat and continue with alternate layers of onions, potatoes and then meat until the casserole is filled. Pour over the marinade, cover, and cook in a moderate oven (180°C, 350°F, mark 4) for a minimum of 1½ hours. Check for tenderness.

Boeuf à l'ancienne

This is a distinctly different boeuf bourguignonne from the more traditional one on page 73. I found it in a book of old Burgundian recipes given to me by a local friend and was surprised to see madeira rather than burgundy being used. It produces a wonderfully aromatic dish. As the original recipe says, 'I leave you to think of the scent which is emitted.'

1–1.25 kg	stewing steak	2–2½ lb
225 g	carrots	½ lb
one	large onion	one
two 5 ml spoons	dried thyme	2 teasp
two	bay leaves	two
two 15 ml spoons	chopped parsley	2 tablesp
two	cloves of garlic	two
two	shallots	two
225 g	mushrooms	½ lb
	salt, pepper	
three 15 ml spoons	brandy	3 tablesp
600 ml	dry madeira	1 pint
75 g	streaky bacon	3 oz
	flour and water paste	

Cut the meat into 5-cm (2-inch) cubes. Slice the carrots, onion and mushrooms finely. In a small flame-proof casserole put a layer of finely-sliced carrots and onion, sprinkle the vegetables with some thyme, crumbled bay leaf and parsley. Place a layer of meat on top and cover with crushed garlic, more onion and chopped shallots. Add the finely-sliced mushrooms. Continue like this until the meat is all finished, seasoning each layer well with salt and pepper. Pour over the brandy and madeira. Place the slices of bacon on top.

Cover the casserole and seal the lid with a flour and water paste. Bring the contents to the boil and then cook the casserole in a very low oven (140°C, 275°F, mark 1) for six hours. Don't raise the lid during cooking. Alternatively, cook the beef all day in a slow electric casserole.

Carbonnade à la flamande

At the risk of offending any Belgian friends, I think this is the one dish which could earn their country a medal in the Gastrolympics.

1–1.25 kg	*stewing beef*	*2–2½ lb*
	oil or butter	
one	*large onion*	*one*
two	*cloves of garlic*	*two*
one 15 ml spoon	*flour*	*1 tablesp*
600 ml	*dark ale*	*1 pint*
	salt, pepper	
one 15 ml spoon	*vinegar*	*1 tablesp*
two 5 ml spoons	*sugar*	*2 teasp*
half 5 ml spoon	*freshly-grated nutmeg*	*½ teasp*

Cut the meat into 5-cm (2-inch) cubes and seal it in the hot fat in a flame-proof casserole. Add the chopped onion and crushed garlic and cook them for a few more minutes. Add the flour and stir well. Pour on the ale and add the other ingredients. Stir well and bring the contents of the casserole to the boil. Cover it, and cook it in a slow oven (150°C, 300°F, mark 2) for two hours. Serve with pureed potatoes.

Boeuf au poivre vert

1–1.25 kg	*stewing beef*	*2–2½ lb*
	oil	
two	*large carrots*	*two*
	salt, pepper	
50 ml	*brandy*	*2 fl oz*
200 ml	*dry white wine*	*7 fl oz*
100 ml	*beef stock (page 214)*	*3 fl oz*
two 5 ml spoons	*green peppercorns*	*2 teasp*

Cut the meat into 5-cm (2-inch) cubes and seal it in the oil. Transfer it to a casserole and add the sliced carrots. Season well. Warm the brandy gently in a soup ladle. Ignite it and pour it over the beef. Add the wine, the stock and the peppercorns.

Cover the casserole and cook it in a slow oven (150°C, 300°F, mark 2) for two hours. The sauce will be rather thin; if you prefer it thicker, add a little beurre manié (page 216). Serve the casserole with noodles.

Boeuf à la bourguignonne

Perhaps no other beef stew has so many adherents or so many variants as Burgundy beef. Some prefer the sauce to be thin, some say you must use genuine burgundy, others insist on the addition of pork, there are those who exclude mushrooms, and so on. The fact is that almost anything goes, as long as it includes beef and red wine. Perhaps the most original variation is boeuf à l'ancienne (page 71).

225 g	button onions	1/2 lb
110 g	streaky bacon	1/4 lb
	oil	
1–1.25 kg	stewing beef	2–2½ lb
two 15 ml spoons	flour	2 tablesp
	salt, pepper	
	marjoram	
	thyme	
175 ml	beef stock (page 214)	6 fl oz
350 ml	full-bodied red wine	12 fl oz
225 g	button mushrooms	1/2 lb

In an oven-proof casserole, fry the whole, peeled onions with the diced bacon and a little oil until they are brown. Take them out and reserve them until later. Cut the meat into 5-cm (2-inch) cubes and seal it in the fat remaining in the pan. (Add more oil if necessary.) When the meat is brown, sprinkle it with the flour, salt, pepper and herbs, and stir well. Add the stock and wine and stir again. Cover, and cook the casserole over a very low heat for three hours, or in a slow oven (150°C, 300°F, mark 2). Keep an eye on the liquid and top it up if necessary, in the same proportion of stock to wine.

After three hours, return the onions to the pan, together with the whole mushrooms, and cook for a further 45 minutes.

The ideal accompaniment is hot French bread and a crisp salad – and of course a good bottle of burgundy.

Boeuf provençale

Capers and anchovy fillets give a piquancy to this Provencal recipe. Herbes de Provence are a mixture of oregano, thyme, rosemary, lavender and other herbs, available pre-packaged in this country.

1–1.25 kg	*stewing beef (in one piece)*	*2–2½ lb*
	olive oil	
three 15 ml spoons	*red wine vinegar*	*3 tablesp*
three 15 ml spoons	*capers*	*3 tablesp*
one 15 ml spoon	*tomato puree*	*1 tablesp*
one 5 ml spoon	*herbes de Provence*	*1 teasp*
two	*cloves of garlic*	*two*
425 ml	*full-bodied red wine*	*14 fl oz*
eight	*anchovy fillets*	*eight*
one	*large bay leaf*	*one*
	salt, pepper	

Seal the beef on all sides in oil. Transfer it to a casserole and add all the remaining ingredients, with the garlic crushed and the anchovies roughly chopped. Cover, and cook in a slow oven (150°C, 300°F, mark 2) for two hours.

Estouffade de boeuf camarguaise

1–1.25 kg	*stewing beef*	*2–2½ lb*
600 ml	*full-bodied red wine*	*1 pint*
one 15 ml spoon	*brandy*	*1 tablesp*
one 5 ml spoon	*herbes de Provence (see above)*	*1 teasp*
	salt, pepper	
110 g	*carrots*	*¼ lb*
110 g	*onions*	*¼ lb*
	olive oil	
50 g	*black olives*	*2 oz*
one	*clove of garlic*	*one*

Cut the meat into 5-cm (2-inch) cubes and marinate it in the wine, brandy, herbs, salt, pepper, sliced carrots and onions for 24 hours. Remove the meat and pat it dry. Seal it in hot oil. Pat the vegetables dry and add them to the meat. Stir them until they are coated with oil and cook them for 15 minutes. Add the marinade, the stoned olives and the crushed garlic. Bring the contents of the pan to the boil, cover it, and simmer it for two hours; or cook it in a moderate oven (160°C, 325°F, mark 3). If you are planning to re-heat the dish, cook it for 1½ hours initially and for a further hour before serving. If you prefer a thicker sauce, add a little beurre manié (page 216).

Beef Stroganoff

I suspect the original version of this popular Russian dish did not include anything alcoholic, but a small amount of madeira would surely help keep out the cold of the Steppes.

700 g	*beef fillet*	*1½ lb*
	salt, pepper	
225 g	*button mushrooms*	*½ lb*
	butter	
one	*large onion*	*one*
two 15 ml spoons	*flour*	*2 tablesp*
300 ml	*beef stock*	*½ pint*
50 ml	*dry madeira*	*2 fl oz*
two 15 ml spoons	*tomato puree*	*2 tablesp*
one 5 ml spoon	*dry mustard*	*1 teasp*
150 ml	*sour cream*	*¼ pint*

Cut the beef into thin strips and season them well. Cook the sliced mushrooms in the butter in a sauté-pan until they are tender. Remove them from the pan and keep them warm. Add the sliced onion and cook it until it is soft. (Add more butter if necessary.) Keep the onion warm with the mushrooms. Add the prepared beef strips and seal them in the hot butter. Remove them and add them to the reserved mushrooms and onion.

Add the flour to the pan and stir until it blends into the butter. Add first the stock and madeira, stirring to make a smooth sauce, then the tomato puree and the mustard. Stir well. Return the meat and vegetables to the sauce, cover the pan and simmer for 20 minutes. Add the sour cream and warm the sauce through.

Substitute sherry for the madeira if you prefer it.

Sicilian beef

The blend of fennel with marsala makes this a particularly aromatic dish. Fennel is one of the few herbs with which I have great success in my garden: it grows despite my efforts. If you are not so fortunate, use dried fennel, but the fresh is obviously preferable.

one	*stick of celery*	*one*
one	*large onion*	*one*
one	*clove of garlic*	*one*
	oil	
1–1.25 kg	*stewing beef*	*2–2½ lb*
two 15 ml spoons	*chopped fresh fennel*	*2 tablesp*
	salt, pepper	
one 15 ml spoon	*flour*	*1 tablesp*
150 ml	*marsala*	*¼ pint*
400 g	*tinned tomatoes*	*14 oz*

In a heavy saucepan or casserole, brown the finely-chopped celery, onion and garlic in the oil. Cut the meat into 5-cm (2-inch) cubes and add it to the pan along with the fennel, salt and pepper. Sprinkle on the flour and stir well. Add the marsala and cook it until the sauce has reduced a little. Add the tomatoes, stir again, and bring the mixture to the boil. Cover the pan and leave it to simmer for about 1½ hours.

Normandy meat-balls

Adding cider and calvados to anything is a virtual guarantee of success – and nowhere better than with minced meat, the advantages of which need no advertisement.

three	*slices of bread*	*three*
450 g	*minced beef*	*1 lb*
225 g	*minced veal*	*½ lb*
one	*medium-sized cooking apple*	*one*
one	*medium-sized onion*	*one*
two	*eggs*	*two*
one 5 ml spoon	*ground mixed spice*	*1 teasp*
one 15 ml spoon	*chopped parsley*	*1 tablesp*
	salt, pepper	
one 15 ml spoon	*flour*	*1 tablesp*
150 ml	*beef stock (page 214)*	*¼ pint*
150 ml	*dry cider*	*¼ pint*
two 15 ml spoons	*single cream*	*2 tablesp*
two 15 ml spoons	*calvados*	*2 tablesp*

Soak the bread in a little water, squeeze out the water, and crumble the bread into the meat along with the grated apple and onion. Add the beaten eggs, mixed spice, parsley, salt and pepper. Mix everything well together and form the mixture into balls, about the size of ping-pong balls. Place them in a shallow oven-dish and bake them, uncovered, in a hot oven (200°C, 400°F, mark 6) for 25 minutes.

Remove the dish from the oven, transferring the meat-balls to a clean oven-proof dish. Return them to the oven, lowering the heat to 150°C (300°F, mark 2).

Pour the fat from the oven-dish into a saucepan and stir in the flour thoroughly. Slowly add the stock and cider and cook until the sauce thickens. Stir in the cream and calvados and warm them through gently. Pour the sauce over the meat-balls and serve them with creamed potatoes.

Lamb

Lamb is something about which we can be very chauvinistic, for there is nothing more delicious than a piece of English lamb, simply roasted. Perhaps the lamb which is served in foreign parts lacks the delicacy of our home-bred variety, and therefore needs dressing up in elaborate disguises. So it is no surprise that many of the recipes in this section come from abroad.

If you have a fine piece of English lamb, you might well prefer to serve it unadorned, roasted on a bed of finely-chopped vegetables. The juices in the pan will provide the basis of an excellent gravy, but a spoonful or so of port, madeira or sherry will give a little lift for minimal effort and expense.

Cordero español

For the non-linguist, this is a leg of lamb, Spanish-style. With sherry, of course.

1.75–2 kg	*leg of lamb*	*3½–4 lb*
two 15 ml spoons	*oil*	*2 tablesp*
	salt, pepper	
one	*large onion*	*one*
175 ml	*dry sherry*	*6 fl oz*
300 ml	*veal or chicken stock (page 215)*	*½ pint*
one	*clove of garlic*	*one*
four 15 ml spoons	*tomato puree*	*4 tablesp*

In a large, heavy casserole, brown the meat in the oil and season it well. Add the sliced onion and cook it until it is golden. Drain off any excess fat. Stir in the sherry and stock and add the crushed garlic and tomato puree. Bring the sauce to the boil. Cover the pan and cook it in a moderate oven (180°C, 350°F, mark 4) for 1½–2 hours.

Remove the meat from the pan and keep it warm. Add a little boiling water to the sauce. Stir it well and bring it to the boil. Let the sauce reduce and thicken a little and serve it with the sliced meat. You could use a lean shoulder of lamb for this recipe.

Casseroled shoulder of lamb

Shoulder of lamb can be sweeter than the leg but is invariably rather fatty. It is a good idea to make this casserole in advance and skim the fat off before re-heating. Choose a casserole with a close-fitting lid, or put a piece of foil under the lid.

110 g	*back bacon*	*¼ lb*
110 g	*lamb's liver*	*¼ lb*
two	*medium-sized onions*	*two*
one	*clove of garlic*	*one*
	chopped parsley	
two	*slices of bread*	*two*
300 ml	*dry white wine*	*½ pint*
	salt, pepper	
1.75 kg (approx.)	*boned shoulder of lamb*	*3½ lb (approx.)*
	oil	
one	*stick of celery*	*one*
one	*carrot*	*one*
two 15 ml spoons	*tomato puree*	*2 tablesp*
300 ml	*water*	*½ pint*

Mix the chopped bacon, liver and one onion with the crushed garlic and parsley. Moisten the bread with a little of the wine and crumble it into the bacon mixture. Season it well and mix everything together. Spread the stuffing on the lamb, roll the meat up and tie it securely. In a flame-proof casserole, brown the meat all over in the oil. Add the remaining chopped onion, the chopped celery and carrot, and the remaining wine. Season the meat well, cover the casserole and cook it in a slow oven (150°C, 300°F, mark 2) for three hours.

Add the tomato puree, mixed with the water, and cook the meat for a further hour, basting and turning it occasionally.

Remove the meat and keep it warm while you skim the fat from the sauce. Serve the meat sliced with the sauce.

Stuffed shoulder of lamb

110 g	dried apricots	1/4 lb
110 g	raisins	1/4 lb
110 g	rice	1/4 lb
one	small onion	one
	oil	
50 g	blanched almonds	2 oz
	salt, pepper	
1.75 kg (approx.)	boned shoulder of lamb	3 1/2 lb (approx.)
225 ml	madeira (sweet or dry)	8 fl oz
50 ml	water	2 fl oz

Soak the coarsely-chopped apricots and the raisins in boiling water. Cook the rice and drain it. Soften the chopped onion in a little oil. Drain the soaked apricots and raisins. Mix together the onion, fruit, rice and roughly-chopped almonds. Season the mixture.

Spread the stuffing on the lamb, roll it up and tie it securely. Place the meat in a roasting-tin, pour in the madeira and season the meat well. Cover the tin with foil and cook the lamb in a moderately slow oven (160°C, 325°F, mark 3) for one hour. Take off the foil and cook the meat for a further hour.

Keep the meat warm while you make the sauce. Skim off the fat, add the water to the tin and bring the sauce to the boil, scraping the bottom of the tin to release the sediment. Carve the meat in thick slices and serve the sauce separately.

Gigot d'agneau à la normande

2 kg (approx.)	leg of lamb	4 lb (approx.)
	salt, pepper	
40 g	butter	1 1/2 oz
150 ml	beef stock (page 214)	1/4 pint
three 15 ml spoons	calvados	3 tablesp
one 5 ml spoon	flour	1 teasp
200 ml	double cream	7 fl oz

Season the lamb. Melt half the butter in a roasting-tin, place the lamb in the tin and cook it, uncovered, in a moderate oven (180°C, 350°F, mark 4) for one hour, basting it from time to time. Remove the lamb and keep it warm. Add the stock and calvados and bring the mixture to the boil, scraping the bottom of the tin to release the sediment. Simmer the sauce for three minutes.

Mix the remaining butter with the flour and add the mixture to the sauce, a little at a time, stirring constantly. Pour in the cream and cook for a further three minutes. Carve the meat and put it on a serving dish. Pour over the sauce.

Leg of lamb with olives

This is an easy, but very tasty, way to prepare a leg of lamb – and a good use for the olives that are invariably left over after a party.

1.75–2 kg	*leg of lamb*	*3½–4 lb*
	salt, pepper	
	oil	
one	*large onion*	*one*
one	*large clove of garlic*	*one*
one 15 ml spoon	*tomato puree*	*1 tablesp*
300 ml	*beef stock (page 214)*	*½ pint*
225 ml	*full-bodied red wine*	*8 fl oz*
175 g	*olives – black, green or mixed*	*6 oz*

Brown the seasoned lamb in the oil in a large, heavy casserole. Add the sliced onion and crushed garlic and soften them. Mix the tomato puree with the stock and pour it over the meat. Cover the pan and cook it in a moderately hot oven (190°C, 375°F, mark 5) for 45 minutes. Add the wine and olives to the meat and return it to the oven, lowered to 180°C (350°F, mark 4) for a further hour.

Remove the meat from the pan and keep it warm. Add a little boiling water to the sauce, stirring well to incorporate the sediment. Serve the sauce with the carved lamb.

Lamb goulash

I always used to think that a goulash had to be made of beef, but since the word 'gulyas' means 'shepherd', it seems quite logical to use lamb.

1–1.25 kg	*boned shoulder of lamb*	*2–2½ lb*
one 15 ml spoon	*oil*	*1 tablesp*
one	*medium-sized onion*	*one*
two	*cloves of garlic*	*two*
two 5 ml spoons	*caraway seeds*	*2 teasp*
two 5 ml spoons	*sweet paprika*	*2 teasp*
four 5 ml spoons	*tomato puree*	*4 teasp*
200 ml	*full-bodied red wine*	*7 fl oz*
200 ml	*stock or water*	*7 fl oz*
	salt, pepper	

Cut the meat into 5-cm (2-inch) cubes, trimming off any excess fat. Brown it in the hot oil. Add the chopped onion, crushed garlic, caraway seeds and paprika. Stir well, and cook the mixture for five minutes. Stir in the tomato puree, wine and stock. Season the goulash and bring it to the boil. Cover it and simmer for 1½ hours.

Serve with boiled potatoes or noodles, and a blob of sour cream, if you wish.

You may prefer to cook this the day before it is required and remove the fat when it has cooled, before re-heating.

Cyprus lamb

This recipe comes from Cyprus where the meat is often served with macaroni and tomato sauce, as well as the potatoes with which it has cooked.

2 kg (approx.)	leg of lamb	4 lb (approx.)
one	lemon	one
two	cloves of garlic	two
six	medium-sized potatoes	six
two	medium-sized onions	two
one	bay leaf	one
one 5 ml spoon	oregano (or half quantity dried)	1 teasp
	salt, pepper	
175 g	tomatoes	6 oz
200 ml	red wine	7 fl oz
150 ml	boiling water	¼ pint

Rub the meat with the cut lemon. Make four or five incisions in it and insert slivers of garlic. Place the meat in a roasting-tin, surrounded by the peeled potatoes and sliced onions. Add the bay leaf and sprinkle the oregano over the meat. Season it well. Lay the skinned, sliced tomatoes on the meat. Pour the wine into the tin and cover it with foil. Cook it in a moderate oven (180°C, 350°F, mark 4) for one hour. Remove the foil and cook the meat for a further 20 minutes. Remove the meat and potatoes from the tin. Add the boiling water to the tin and heat it, scraping the onions and sediment from the bottom. Bring the sauce to the boil and serve it with the sliced meat.

Daube de Provence

It seems odd to me that herbs which I associate with the South of France are almost the only ones to flourish in my northern garden, but rosemary, thyme and bay are there in abundance so I happily use them for this Provencal dish.

450 g	*boned shoulder of lamb*	*1 lb*
450 g	*boned shoulder of pork*	*1 lb*
	oil	
one	*large onion*	*one*
two	*leeks*	*two*
two	*cloves of garlic*	*two*
400 g	*tinned tomatoes*	*14 oz*
	(or equivalent of fresh)	
450 ml	*full-bodied red wine*	*¾ pint*
one	*sprig of rosemary*	*one*
two	*sprigs of thyme*	*two*
one	*large bay leaf*	*one*
	salt, pepper	

Cut the meat into 5-cm (2-inch) cubes and brown them in the oil. Peel and chop the onion and leeks and add them to the pan. Add the crushed garlic and cook, stirring well, until the vegetables begin to colour. Add the remaining ingredients and bring the mixture to the boil. Cover the pan and cook it in a slow oven (150°C, 300°F, mark 2) for two hours.

You could use *either* lamb *or* pork if you prefer.

Spaghetti con sugo d'agnello

Spaghetti bolognese is so popular that we possibly tend to ignore the many other sauces there are to accompany pasta. This lamb sauce makes an interesting change.

four 15 ml spoons	*olive oil*	*4 tablesp*
one	*large clove of garlic*	*one*
one	*bay leaf*	*one*
1 kg	*boneless lamb*	*2 lb*
	salt, pepper	
one	*pinch of chilli powder*	*one*
200 ml	*dry white wine*	*7 fl oz*
450 g	*fresh tomatoes*	*1 lb*
two	*green or red peppers*	*two*
450 g	*spaghetti*	*1 lb*
	grated Parmesan	

Heat the oil and add the crushed garlic and bay leaf. Dice the lamb; combine it with the salt, pepper and chilli powder. Stir it into the oil and when it begins to brown, add half the wine. Let it evaporate before adding the peeled and quartered tomatoes and sliced peppers. Add the remainder of the wine and cook the sauce over a low heat until the meat is tender (about 30 minutes). If more liquid is required, add a little beef stock.

Boil the spaghetti *al dente*. Strain it and return it to the pan. Add the sauce and stir it through the pasta. Serve the spaghetti with grated Parmesan.

Loin of lamb

A loin of lamb is quite a dramatic-looking joint and this recipe makes a fine dinner-party dish. This size of loin should serve four very generously, five quite well and six somewhat parsimoniously. You could apply the same treatment to a saddle of lamb, which would feed eight to ten. Increase the amount of marinade by half.

2 kg (approx.)	*loin of lamb*	*4 lb (approx.)*
300 ml	*full-bodied red wine*	*½ pint*
two 15 ml spoons	*tomato puree*	*2 tablesp*
two	*cloves of garlic*	*two*
one	*sprig of rosemary*	*one*
	salt, pepper	

Ask the butcher to chine the lamb and remove any spare fat. Mix together the wine, tomato puree, crushed garlic, rosemary and salt and pepper, making sure the puree is dissolved. Put the lamb into a roasting-tin and pour over the marinade. Leave the lamb for three hours, turning it from time to time. Cook it (in the marinade), uncovered, in a moderate oven (180°C, 350°F, mark 4) for one hour, or slightly less if you prefer your lamb pink.

Remove the lamb from the pan and carefully skim off the fat. Add a cup of boiling water to the pan and stir well to incorporate the sediment. Bring the sauce to the boil.

Veal

Veal goes well with all the different ingredients of our 'kitchen cellar' – a natural with spirits such as calvados and brandy, a dream with marsala wine, surprisingly good with beer.

It is a sad fact that fewer and fewer butchers are selling veal these days, and certainly the price of this most delicate of meats has contributed to their reluctance to offer it to customers. There are one or two ways to economise. It is possible, with the help of a friendly butcher, to buy pieces of veal cut from the fillet but too small to use as proper escalopes. These smaller 'off-cuts' are perfectly satisfactory for many dishes which call for escalopes. Do not confuse this cut with 'pie veal' which is for stewing and would be far too tough to use for recipes requiring fillet.

Pork fillet is a little less expensive than veal and is quite suitable as a substitute in almost any veal recipe. Indeed it is quite a common practice on the Continent to list 'schnitzel' on a menu and unless it specifies veal, the meat is almost bound to be pork, cooked in the same way as veal.

Another less expensive substitute in many of these recipes could be turkey fillet, which is quite easily found in supermarkets as well as butchers' shops.

Scaloppini al marsala

Nutty marsala combines admirably with veal in this classic Sicilian recipe. Scaloppini are small escalopes, so there is no need to use the more expensive pieces of fillet.

700 g	off-cuts of veal fillet	1½ lb
	flour	
	salt, pepper	
	butter	
100 ml	veal or chicken stock (page 215)	3 fl oz
175 ml	marsala	6 fl oz

Pass the veal slices through the seasoned flour and brown them in the hot butter. Cook the meat for about three minutes on each side, depending on the thickness. Remove the meat from the pan and keep it warm. Add the stock and marsala and bring the liquid to the boil. Simmer until it has reduced by half. Add a spoonful of butter, stir well and pour the sauce over the veal.

Orange roast veal

1.75 kg (approx.)	leg of veal	3½ lb (approx.)
	oil	
	salt, pepper	
175 ml	red wine	6 fl oz
175 ml	veal or beef stock (page 214)	6 fl oz
175 ml	orange juice	6 fl oz
one 15 ml spoon	Grand Marnier	1 tablesp
	or other orange liqueur	

Rub the veal with oil and season it well. Place it in a roasting-tin and pour over the wine, stock and orange juice. Cook it, uncovered, in a moderately slow oven (160°C, 325°F, mark 3) for about 1¾ hours, basting it frequently. Remove the meat from the pan and keep it warm. Add a little water to the juices and scrape the sediment from the bottom of the pan. Bring the sauce to the boil, add the Grand Marnier and stir it well. Serve the sauce with the sliced veal.

If you like, you can cut some orange peel into thin matchsticks, blanch the pieces in boiling water and add them to the sauce.

Veal with prunes

It is such a pity prunes bring back memories of schooldays when served, soggily, with lumpy custard. There's no such thought about this rather more sophisticated treatment of what is a most tasty fruit.

1.25 kg	*pie veal*	*2½ lb*
	flour	
	oil or butter	
one	*large onion*	*one*
one	*clove of garlic*	*one*
300 ml	*water*	*½ pint*
300 ml	*red wine*	*½ pint*
225 g	*pitted prunes*	*½ lb*
	salt, pepper	

Pass the cubed veal through the flour and brown it in a heavy casserole in the hot oil. Add the sliced onion and crushed garlic and cook them for a few minutes until they are lightly coloured. Add the water and wine, stir everything well, and bring the mixture to the boil. Add the prunes and seasoning. Cover the casserole and cook it in a slow oven (150°C, 300°F, mark 2) for two hours. Serve it with a green salad and French bread.

Stuffed veal escalopes

There's no escape from using full-sized escalopes here to accommodate the stuffing – but remember that turkey escalopes work well (page 87).

four–six	*large escalopes*	*four–six*
two	*medium-sized onions*	*two*
	butter	
110 g	*ham*	*¼ lb*
25 g	*breadcrumbs*	*1 oz*
one	*egg*	*one*
four 5 ml spoons	*fresh mixed herbs*	*4 teasp*
	(or half quantity dried)	
200 ml	*dry white wine*	*7 fl oz*
200 ml	*veal or chicken stock (page 215)*	*7 fl oz*
one	*sliver of lemon peel*	*one*
	salt, pepper	

Ask your butcher to beat the veal out as thinly as possible – or do it yourself between sheets of plastic wrap or grease-proof paper.

To make the stuffing, soften one finely-chopped onion in hot butter. Add the finely-chopped ham, the breadcrumbs, the beaten egg and the herbs. Mix everything together well. Spread the stuffing on the escalopes, roll them up and secure them with toothpicks or cotton.

Slice the second onion and soften it in butter. Add the rolled escalopes and brown them all over. Pour over the wine and stock. Add the lemon peel, salt and pepper. Cover the pan and leave it to simmer for 30 minutes.

If the sauce needs thickening, add a little beurre manié (page 216). Remove the toothpicks or cotton before serving.

Veal escalopes with vermouth

The light herby flavour of vermouth is an excellent foil to the delicacy of veal, as is shown in this recipe and in the casserole of veal with vermouth (page 96).

six	*rashers of bacon*	*six*
	butter	
one	*large clove of garlic*	*one*
one	*medium-sized onion*	*one*
four–six	*veal escalopes*	*four–six*
	flour	
	salt, pepper	
200 ml	*dry white vermouth*	*7 fl oz*
200 ml	*veal or chicken stock (page 215)*	*7 fl oz*

Fry the chopped bacon in a little butter until it is crisp. Add the crushed garlic and finely-chopped onion and cook them until they are soft. Remove the mixture from the pan and keep it warm.

Pass the veal through the seasoned flour. Fry it until it is tender, adding more butter if required. Remove the meat and keep it warm. Return the onion mixture to the pan. Add the vermouth and stock and stir well to scrape the sediment from the bottom of the pan. Season to taste. Simmer for a few minutes to reduce the sauce if desired. Pour it over the meat.

If a thicker sauce is preferred you can add a little beurre manié (page 216).

Scaloppini al pomidoro

This is a useful dish to make, with the sort of ingredients you are bound to have to hand. Scaloppini are small escalopes (see page 88).

two	*medium-sized onions*	*two*
	oil	
400 g	*tinned tomatoes*	*14 oz*
	(or 450 g/1 lb of fresh)	
two 5 ml spoons	*fresh basil*	*2 teasp*
	(or half quantity dried)	
one 5 ml spoon	*sugar*	*1 teasp*
one	*sliver of orange peel*	*one*
one 15 ml spoon	*tomato puree*	*1 tablesp*
200 ml	*red wine*	*7 fl oz*
	salt, pepper	
700 g	*off-cuts of veal fillet*	*1½ lb*
	flour	
two	*eggs*	*two*
	fresh, white breadcrumbs	

Soften the sliced onions in the hot oil. Add the tomatoes (skinned and sliced if using fresh), the basil, sugar, orange peel, tomato puree, wine and seasonings. Bring the sauce to the boil, reduce the heat, and let it simmer gently while you cook the veal.

Pass the pieces of veal first through the flour, then through the beaten eggs, and finally through the breadcrumbs. Fry the prepared veal in hot oil for about four minutes on each side.

Serve the veal very hot, with the sauce separate.

Osso buco milanese

This classic Italian dish derives its exceptionally aromatic flavour from the combination of vegetables and lemon rind in which it is cooked, and the last-minute addition of gremolata, a mixture of chopped parsley, garlic, and lemon and orange rind.

six	*pieces of shin of veal (at least 5 cm/2 inches thick)*	*six*
	seasoned flour	
	oil or butter	
one	*medium-sized onion*	*one*
one	*carrot*	*one*
one	*stick of celery*	*one*
two	*cloves of garlic*	*two*
three	*sprigs of marjoram (or the equivalent of dried)*	*three*
one	*small piece of lemon rind*	*one*
300 ml	*dry white wine*	*½ pint*
four	*large ripe tomatoes*	*four*
450 ml	*veal or beef stock (page 214)*	*¾ pint*
two 5 ml spoons	*chopped parsley*	*2 teasp*
one 5 ml spoon	*grated orange rind*	*1 teasp*
one 5 ml spoon	*grated lemon rind*	*1 teasp*

Pass the pieces of veal through the seasoned flour and brown them in the hot oil or butter. Finely chop the onion, carrot, celery and one clove of garlic and add these to the meat with the marjoram and the piece of lemon rind. (Keep the bones upright so that the marrow stays in place.) Cook this mixture for two minutes and then add the wine. Simmer until the wine has almost evaporated. Add the peeled, de-seeded and chopped tomatoes, the stock, and more salt and pepper if required. Cover the pan and simmer for one hour. Ten minutes before the meat is cooked, remove the lid and raise the heat to reduce the liquid a little. Crush the remaining garlic and mix it with the chopped parsley and finely-grated orange and lemon rind. Sprinkle this mixture on top of the osso buco just before serving.

Osso buco is traditionally served with risotto milanese (page 47).

Fillet of veal Jerez

The sauce in this recipe resembles a zabaglione, which may sound strange, but it tastes very delicate and unusual. Since it deflates very rapidly, have your guests sitting and waiting . . . in happy anticipation.

700 g	off-cuts of veal fillet	1½ lb
50 g	butter	2 oz
50 g	button mushrooms	2 oz
one	shallot or small onion	one
200 g	tinned sweet pimento	7 oz
125 ml	single cream	4 fl oz
two	egg yolks	two
125 ml	dry sherry	4 fl oz
	salt, pepper	

Toss the pieces of veal in half the butter over a high heat. Remove them from the pan when cooked and keep warm. Add the remaining butter, sliced mushrooms, finely-chopped shallot and sliced pimento to the pan. Season them well and cook them for three minutes. Add the cream and bring it to the boil. Return the meat to the pan, cover, and reduce the heat.

Put the egg yolks and sherry in a bowl over a pan of hot water. Whisk the mixture until it is frothy. Add it to the veal and stir gently.

Adjust the seasoning and serve the veal immediately. Noodles or rice go well with this dish.

Sauté de veau au cidre

1.25 kg	*pie veal*	*2½ lb*
	oil	
two	*medium-sized onions*	*two*
two	*shallots*	*two*
one	*bouquet garni (page 216)*	*one*
	salt, pepper	
450 ml	*dry cider*	*¾ pint*
25 g	*butter*	*1 oz*
25 g	*flour*	*1 oz*
150 ml	*single cream*	*¼ pint*
half	*lemon*	*half*

Cube the veal and brown it in the hot oil. Add the finely-chopped onions and shallots, the bouquet garni, and salt and pepper. Moisten the veal with a glass of the cider, cover the pan, and simmer it gently for about one hour.

While the meat is cooking make the sauce. Make a roux (page 217) with the butter and flour. Add the rest of the cider all at once and beat it well with a whisk. Cook it until the sauce is smooth and thick. Add the cream and season to taste. Bring the sauce to the boil and add the juice of half a lemon. When the meat is cooked, stir the sauce into it.

Veal paprika

one	*large onion*	*one*
	oil or butter	
1–1.25 kg	*pie veal*	*2–2½ lb*
	flour	
	salt, pepper	
two 15 ml spoons	*sweet paprika*	*2 tablesp*
300 ml	*fruity white wine*	*½ pint*
225 g	*button mushrooms*	*½ lb*
150 ml	*sour cream*	*¼ pint*

Soften the sliced onion in the hot oil or butter. Pass the cubed meat through the seasoned flour and add it to the onion. Lightly brown the meat. Add the paprika and stir it in well. Cook the mixture for three minutes. Add the wine, stir again, cover the pan, and simmer it for 1¼ hours. Add the whole mushrooms and cook for a further 15 minutes. Stir in the sour cream and warm it through.

Serve the veal with noodles – green ones look particularly pretty with the pink sauce.

Veal and vermouth casserole

one	large onion	one
	oil or butter	
1 kg	pie veal	2 lb
	flour	
	salt, pepper	
175 g	button mushrooms	6 oz
110 g	streaky bacon	¼ lb
300 ml	veal or chicken stock (page 215)	½ pint
150 ml	dry white vermouth	¼ pint
two 15 ml spoons	lemon juice	2 tablesp
	lemon rind	
two 15 ml spoons	single cream	2 tablesp

Soften the sliced onion in the hot fat in a flame-proof casserole. Pass the cubed veal through the seasoned flour. Brown the veal. Add the whole mushrooms and chopped bacon. Cook for three minutes. Stir in the stock, vermouth, lemon juice and a little grated rind. Check the seasoning.

Bring the mixture to the boil and then reduce the heat, cover the pan, and simmer for one hour (or cook in a moderate oven [180°C, 350°F, mark 4]).

Stir in the cream just before serving.

Veal and ale

The sauce of this dish is rich and spicy, a good contrast to the blandness of the meat.

two	*medium-sized onions*	*two*
	oil	
1 kg	*pie veal*	*2 lb*
	flour	
	salt, pepper	
225 g	*tinned tomatoes*	*½ lb*
one	*bay leaf*	*one*
half 5 ml spoon	*ground cloves*	*½ teasp*
one 5 ml spoon	*fresh marjoram*	*1 teasp*
	(or half quantity dried)	
one	*pinch of cayenne pepper*	*one*
450 ml	*light ale*	*¾ pint*
four	*gingersnaps*	*four*

Soften the sliced onions in the hot oil. Pass the veal through seasoned flour and add it to the onions. Brown the meat. Add the remaining ingredients, except for the biscuits.

Bring the mixture to the boil, reduce the heat, cover the pan and simmer it for one hour. Add the crushed biscuits and cook for a further 30 minutes.

Serve the veal with mashed or pureed potatoes.

Pork and ham

Roast pork and apple sauce, cold ham carved from the bone: these are the images conjured up by pork and ham. But there are also some very enticing and adventurous ways to cook pork. Cider is a natural partner, but try it too in the Italian style, al marsala, or the Alsace way, with sauerkraut. There's a selection from various other styles of cooking, with sugar and spice and all things nice.

A piece of gammon can be the key to quite an economical meal, and even ready-cooked sliced ham can be treated to some delicious sauces to provide a more substantial – and more interesting – dinner-party dish. And reasonably-priced bacon joints or sausages make tasty dishes too.

Pork casserole

1–1.25 kg	*stewing pork*	*2–2½ lb*
	flour	
	salt, pepper	
	pork fat	
110 g	*carrots*	*¼ lb*
two	*leeks*	*two*
one	*sprig of rosemary*	*one*
600 ml	*veal or chicken stock (page 215)*	*1 pint*
300 ml	*dry (or rough) cider*	*½ pint*
one	*large cooking apple*	*one*

Pass the cubed pork through the seasoned flour. Melt the fat and toss the cubes in it to brown them. Put them into a casserole, together with the sliced carrots and leeks. Strip the rosemary from its stalk and add it to the meat with the stock, cider and peeled and sliced apple.

Season the casserole well, cover it, and either cook it in a slow oven (140°C, 275°F, mark 1) for three hours or cook it for two hours and then reheat it for a further two hours the following day.

Costa di maiale al marsala

The unique flavour of marsala, the tangy taste of citrus, and some herbs and spices, all combine to make this an intriguing dish.

150 ml	marsala	¼ pint
two	oranges	two
one	clove of garlic	one
one	small sprig of rosemary	one
one	pinch of cinnamon	one
	salt, pepper	
six	pork chops	six
	oil	

Make a marinade with the marsala, the juice of the oranges and a little grated rind, the crushed garlic, rosemary, cinnamon, salt and pepper. Mix everything together well and leave the chops to marinate for at least one hour. Remove the chops from the marinade, pat them dry and brown them in the hot fat. Drain off the excess fat. Pour over the marinade, cover the pan, and simmer the contents for about one hour.

Maiale ubriaco

The name, translated as 'drunken pork', conjures up lovely pictures in my mind of a lurching porker, staggering around the farmyard. You can adapt the recipe to use pork chops if you prefer.

2 kg (approx.)	leg of pork	4 lb (approx.)
	salt, pepper	
two 15 ml spoons	olive oil	2 tablesp
two	cloves of garlic	two
600 ml	red wine	1 pint
	chopped parsley	
two	lemons	two

Season the meat well. Heat the oil with the crushed garlic in a large flame-proof casserole and seal the meat on all sides. Pour on the wine, bring it to the boil, reduce the heat, cover the casserole, and simmer it for 2½ hours. Take out the meat, sprinkle it with the chopped parsley and garnish with quartered lemons. Serve the sauce separately.

Pork chops with coriander

Coriander is not widely used, but those who know it will appreciate its beautiful lemony aroma. It is worth grinding the seeds freshly to get the full pungency.

six	pork chops	six
	salt, pepper	
	oil	
150 ml	red wine	5 fl oz
two 15 ml spoons	ground coriander	2 tablesp

Trim the chops, season them well, and fry them on both sides in hot oil in a flame-proof casserole until they begin to change colour. Add the wine and coriander. Cover the casserole and cook it in a moderate oven (180°C, 350°F, mark 4) for 45 minutes, until the meat is cooked and the liquid almost all absorbed.

Pork and cabbage casserole

The combination of brown sugar and cider gives this casserole a very rich flavour.

25 g	cooking fat	1 oz
1 kg	stewing pork	2 lb
one	large onion	one
750 g	white cabbage	1½ lb
50 g	raisins	2 oz
25 g	brown sugar	1 oz
	salt, pepper	
300 ml	dry cider	½ pint
450 g	cooking apples	1 lb

Heat the fat in a flame-proof casserole, and brown the pork, either cut into 5-cm (2-inch) cubes or in one piece. Remove the meat, and soften the sliced onion and cabbage in the fat. Add the raisins and sugar and stir them well. Put the browned meat on top of the cabbage, season with salt and pepper, and pour over the cider. Cover the pan, and cook it in a warm oven (160°C, 325°F, mark 3) for 2¼ hours. Add the peeled and sliced apples and cook the casserole for a further 15 minutes.

Serve it with rice or noodles.

Sauerkraut and sausages

This Alsace dish may not be the most sophisticated, but it is certainly very tasty. It is easily expandable with the addition of more (and different varieties of) sausages.

700 g	*sauerkraut (fresh or tinned)*	*1½ lb*
one 15 ml spoon	*butter or lard*	*1 tablesp*
one	*large onion*	*one*
one	*small ham knuckle*	*one*
225 g	*salt pork*	*½ lb*
110 g	*bacon in one piece*	*¼ lb*
150 ml	*beef stock (page 214)*	*¼ pint*
300 ml	*dry white wine*	*½ pint*
five	*juniper berries*	*five*
three	*cloves of garlic*	*three*
three	*bratwursts*	*three*
four	*knackwursts*	*four*
six	*frankfurters*	*six*

Wash and drain the sauerkraut. Brown the sliced onion in the butter in a heavy flame-proof casserole. Remove the dish from the heat and put the sauerkraut on top of the onions. Add the ham knuckle, the salt pork and the bacon. Stir in the stock, wine, juniper berries and crushed garlic.

Cover the casserole, and cook it in a very slow oven (140°C, 275°F, mark 1) for three hours. Carefully remove the meat and discard the fat. Cut the meat into chunks and return it to the casserole. Add the whole sausages, cover the casserole, and return it to the oven for a further hour. Add a little more stock and wine if required: there should just be enough to moisten it – it should not be swimming in liquid.

Serve with boiled potatoes. Cut the larger sausages in half before serving.

If you can get freshly-made sauerkraut from a delicatessen, it is much better than the tinned variety.

Be prepared to have thirsty guests after this spicy, but very delicious, meal.

Parson's Stew

You may find it odd that a dish from Bulgaria is called Parson's Stew, but no doubt it is still made there, by party functionaries as well as priests.

750 g	button onions	1½ lb
two	cloves of garlic	two
50 g	cooking fat	2 oz
1 kg	lean stewing pork	2 lb
	salt, pepper	
one 5 ml spoon	paprika	1 teasp
two	bay leaves	two
one 15 ml spoon	tomato puree	1 tablesp
one 15 ml spoon	flour	1 tablesp
200 ml	dry white wine	7 fl oz

Peel the onions and garlic and brown them in the hot fat. Remove them from the pan and put in the pork, cut into 2.5-cm (one-inch) cubes. Brown the meat and season it well with the salt, pepper and paprika. Add enough water to cover the meat, bring it to the boil, cover the pan, and simmer it for 15 minutes. Return the onions and garlic to the pan, together with the bay leaves. Continue to simmer the stew for a further 45 minutes.

Mix the tomato puree, flour and wine together and stir the mixture into the pan. Cook gently until the sauce is thick, adding a little more water if necessary.

Pork chops with apples and corn

six	pork chops	six
	salt, pepper	
	oil	
four	eating apples	four
350 g	corn kernels (fresh, frozen or tinned)	¾ lb
300 ml	dry cider	½ pint
100 ml	single cream	3 fl oz

Brown the trimmed and seasoned chops in the oil. Remove the chops and keep them warm. Peel and slice the apples, add them to the pan, and allow them to soften. Stir the corn (drain it if you are using tinned) into the apples. Return the chops to the pan, add the cider, cover the pan, and simmer the contents for about 40 minutes, or until the meat is tender. Remove the chops from the pan, add the cream and warm it through, stirring constantly. Pour the sauce over the chops.

Pork chops niçoise

Anything 'niçoise' goes in my kitchen, bringing a whiff of the South of France with it. This recipe could also be used for veal chops.

six	*pork chops*	*six*
	flour	
	salt, pepper	
	olive oil or butter	
one	*large onion*	*one*
two	*shallots (optional)*	*two*
one	*large clove of garlic*	*one*
450 g	*ripe tomatoes*	*1 lb*
one	*large green pepper*	*one*
two 15 ml spoons	*tomato puree*	*2 tablesp*
one 15 ml spoon	*chopped tarragon or basil (or the equivalent of dried)*	*1 tablesp*
150 ml	*dry white wine*	*¼ pint*

Trim the chops and pass them through the seasoned flour. Brown them in the hot oil or butter. Remove them from the pan and keep them warm. Add the chopped onion and shallots and the crushed garlic to the pan and cook them for one minute. Add the tomatoes, peeled, chopped and de-seeded, the sliced pepper, the tomato puree and the herbs. Season well, and pour over the wine. Place the chops on top of the vegetables, cover the pan, and simmer the contents for 40 minutes or cook in a moderate oven (180°C, 350°F, mark 4).

Pork fillet with mushrooms

A Danish friend introduced me to pork fillet, showing me an amazing number of different ways of preparing it. Here's one version.

700 g–1 kg	*pork fillet*	*1½–2 lb*
	butter	
	salt, pepper	
one 5 ml spoon	*dried oregano*	*1 teasp*
150 ml	*fruity white wine*	*¼ pint*
one 15 ml spoon	*tomato puree*	*1 tablesp*
225 g	*button mushrooms*	*½ lb*
150 ml	*single cream*	*¼ pint*

Cut the pork into slices about 2.5 cm (one inch) thick and beat them flat (or ask the butcher to make escalopes from the fillet). Brown the meat in the butter in a sauté-pan. Season it well and add the oregano, wine and tomato puree. Cover the pan and simmer the contents for 20 minutes. Add the sliced mushrooms and cook them for five minutes. Add the cream and warm it through gently. Check the seasoning before serving.

Ham in cream sauce

450 g	*cooked ham, thinly sliced*	*1 lb*
175 ml	*dry sherry*	*6 fl oz*
25 g	*butter*	*1 oz*
one 15 ml spoon	*flour*	*1 tablesp*
150 ml	*single cream*	*¼ pint*
	pepper	
110 g	*grated Gruyère*	*¼ lb*

Marinate the ham in the sherry for three or four hours. Take it out of the marinade, pat it dry, and warm it in the hot butter. Remove it from the pan and keep it warm. Add the flour to the pan, and stir it well, off the heat, to make a smooth paste. Add the sherry and return the pan to the heat. Stir in the cream and some freshly-ground pepper. Stir the sauce well and pour it over the ham.

Sprinkle the grated cheese on top and brown it under the grill for a minute or two.

Jambon vendangeur

This quickly-made recipe from the Arbois district of France is a useful idea for unexpected guests. You could, at a pinch, use tinned ham, though freshly-cooked ham, or at least ham cut from the bone, is preferable.

25 g	butter	1 oz
one 15 ml spoon	flour	1 tablesp
175 ml	fruity white wine	6 fl oz
two	cloves	two
two	bay leaves	two
175 g	green grapes	6 oz
	salt, pepper	
450 g	cooked ham	1 lb

Melt the butter and stir in the flour. Slowly add the wine, stirring to make a smooth sauce. Add the cloves, bay leaves and grapes, halved and de-seeded. (You can peel them if you have the time, but I don't think it is necessary.) Season with salt and pepper, remembering that the ham is likely to be salty. Add the ham, either cut into chunks or, if it is sliced, rolled up. Warm the ham through and serve it immediately.

Cider and honey gammon

The gammon looks rather like a hedgehog when it emerges from the oven with its firm crust. This is a succulent way to cook it and makes a tasty meal.

1.5–2 kg	gammon	3–4 lb
110 g	brown breadcrumbs	¼ lb
two 15 ml spoons	brown sugar	2 tablesp
300 ml	medium-sweet cider	½ pint
two 15 ml spoons	honey	2 tablesp

Cover the gammon with water and boil it for one hour. Remove it from the water and peel away the skin and some of the fat, leaving a thin layer on the meat. Mix the breadcrumbs and sugar together, and add a spoonful of the cider to bind the mixture. Press the crumbs onto the gammon, patting them down firmly. Place the gammon in a shallow oven-dish. Warm the cider and honey gently to dissolve the honey. Pour this mixture into the dish, round the gammon.

Cook the gammon, uncovered, in a moderately hot oven (190°C, 375°F, mark 5) for 1½ hours, basting it from time to time. The liquid will be absorbed by the breadcrumb mixture, which firms up as the joint is cooking and provides a delicious crust to be eaten with the thickly-sliced gammon.

Jambon persillé

This Burgundian speciality always seemed to me to be very complicated to make at home. In fact it is quite easy and the resulting dish looks and tastes lovely, and should feed six more than generously.

1.5 kg	*unsmoked boiling bacon (hock)*	*3 lb*
two	*bay leaves*	*two*
one 5 ml spoon	*peppercorns*	*1 teasp*
six	*cloves*	*six*
one	*strip of lemon peel*	*one*
two	*cloves of garlic*	*two*
three	*parsley stalks*	*three*
300 ml	*dry white wine*	*½ pint*
one	*large bunch of parsley*	*one*
one 15 ml spoon	*gelatine*	*1 tablesp*

Cover the bacon with water and bring it to the boil. Pour off the water and add all the remaining ingredients except the bunch of parsley and the gelatine. Add water just to cover. Bring it to the boil and then reduce the heat, cover the pan, and simmer it for two hours.

Remove the bacon from the pan, discard the skin and fat and cut the bacon into small pieces. Strain the stock and measure 560 ml (1 pint). Sprinkle the gelatine over the stock and return it to the pan. Heat to dissolve the gelatine. Chop the parsley very finely (use a food processor or liquidiser for speed) and put it into a pudding basin or charlotte mould. Add the cut-up bacon and mix it with the parsley before pouring on the stock and gelatine mixture. Mix the liquid in thoroughly.

Leave the mixture to cool before refrigerating, covered, preferably overnight. Turn out the contents when they have set firm and serve either as an hors d'oeuvre or main course. It makes an attractive part of a cold buffet.

Poultry

Chicken and turkey are wonderfully versatile bases on which to build dishes both simple and exotic. There are of course many classic recipes for chicken, some of which I have altered a little to my own taste.

Turkey has now become an all-the-year-round bird, not just one for the festive season. A recent feature of the poultry scene has been the marketing of a wide variety of different cuts and this has provided a very useful service – no longer need you be left with a lot of dark meat if you are a white-meat family. Fillets of turkey can be cooked in a fraction of the time that meat on the bone would take.

With chickens too you can buy almost any individual cut you like – drumsticks or wings, halved or quartered birds and breasts, all ready for cooking in any way you choose.

Duck is quite an extravagant bird compared with turkey and chicken, both of which are very good value. Unfortunately, with the best will in the world you may find it hard to get more than four portions out of one duck, however large it is, since it sometimes seems to be all bone and fat. I have solved the problem, when cooking duck for a dinner party, by buying individual portions, which are now fairly well distributed in supermarkets and freezer stores. It has the advantage of ensuring that there will be enough to go round, and perhaps even more important, you save that last-minute struggle carving the right number of portions. If you want to cook a duck whole, one 2.5 kg/5 lb duck will serve four quite well, but for larger numbers I would recommend using individual portions.

Roast chicken

A chicken simply roasted with just a little liquor added is as easy as falling off a log, and much more fun.

	butter	
2–2.25 kg	*roasting chicken*	*4–4½ lb*
	salt, pepper	
125 ml	*dry sherry or madeira*	*4 fl oz*

Butter the well-seasoned chicken and roast it in a moderate oven (180°C, 350°F, mark 4) for 1½ hours. Twenty minutes before the chicken is ready, remove it from the oven and keep it warm.

Drain off most of the fat and add the sherry or madeira. Scrape the bottom of the pan to release the sediment and bring the liquid to the boil. Return the chicken to the pan and replace it in the oven for a further 20 minutes cooking, basting it frequently.

This recipe is equally effective with brandy: use only 50 ml (2 fl oz).

Chicken cider casserole

This English cider recipe is not quite as rich as its French counterparts since it does not include masses of thick cream, for which cholesterol-watchers will no doubt be grateful.

2–2.25 kg	*roasting chicken*	*4–4½ lb*
	flour	
	salt, pepper	
	oil and/or butter	
one	*large onion*	*one*
450 ml	*dry cider*	*¾ pint*
one	*green pepper*	*one*
225 g	*tomatoes*	*½ lb*

Roll the chicken in seasoned flour and brown it all over in the hot fat. Remove it to a casserole and brown the chopped onion in the fat. Add one 15 ml (table) spoon of flour to the pan, stirring well. Pour in the cider slowly, stirring until the sauce is smooth. Pour it over the chicken, add the chopped and de-seeded pepper and season it well.

Cover the casserole and cook it in a moderate oven (180°C, 350°F, mark 4) for 1¼ hours. Skin, chop and de-seed the tomatoes and add them to the casserole. Cook it for a further 15 minutes.

Mrs Thatcher's chicken

This recipe emanated from 'Number 10' and is a Thatcher family favourite. Since you get a good chicken soup from it as well, you could say it is something of an economic miracle.

2–2.25 kg	*roasting chicken*	*4–4½ lb*
one	*carrot*	*one*
two	*sticks of celery*	*two*
one	*medium-sized onion*	*one*
one	*leek*	*one*
	salt, pepper	
two	*egg yolks*	*two*
300 ml	*single cream*	*½ pint*
125 ml	*dry sherry*	*4 fl oz*
	grated lemon rind	

Cook the chicken the day before you require it as it is best left overnight in its sauce.

Place the chicken in a large pan and add the chopped carrot, celery, onion, leek and plenty of salt and pepper. Bring everything to the boil and then reduce the heat, cover, and simmer the chicken for 1½ hours, or until it is tender. Remove it from the pan and reserve the stock for use as soup. Cut the chicken into large pieces, discarding the skin, and lay them in a shallow dish.

To make the sauce, mix together in a small, heavy pan the egg yolks, cream, sherry, salt and pepper. Stir the sauce over a very low heat (or use a double-boiler, page 216) until it just begins to thicken. Do not allow it to boil. Pour the sauce over the chicken. Sprinkle the finely-grated lemon rind on top and leave it to cool overnight. You will find that the sauce thickens as it cools.

Coq au vin

By using the generalisation of 'vin' rather than specifying which wine, I leave it to you to use whatever red wine you choose, whether by preference or pocket, or both. In an ideal world you would use a wine from Burgundy, and more particularly a Chambertin . . .

six	*chicken joints*	*six*
	flour	
50 g	*butter*	*2 oz*
110 g	*bacon*	*¼ lb*
350 g	*button onions*	*¾ lb*
two	*cloves of garlic*	*two*
one 5 ml spoon	*fresh thyme*	*1 teasp*
	(or half quantity dried)	
one 15 ml spoon	*chopped parsley*	*1 tablesp*
	salt, pepper	
50 ml	*brandy*	*2 fl oz*
300 ml	*full-bodied red wine*	*½ pint*
350 g	*button mushrooms*	*¾ lb*

In a heavy pan, brown the floured chicken joints well in the melted butter. Add the chopped bacon, whole peeled onions, crushed garlic and herbs. Season well. Cook over a moderate heat for five minutes.

Warm the brandy in a soup ladle, ignite it and pour it over the chicken. When the flames have subsided, add the wine. Cover the pan, and simmer the chicken for about one hour, or cook it in a slow oven (150°C, 300°F, mark 2). Add the whole mushrooms and cook the chicken for a further half-hour.

Serve with slices of fried bread and a crisp green salad.

If you prefer, as I do, to cook this the day before, add the mushrooms before reheating. This dish freezes well and makes a good party meal.

Chicken in ale

six	*chicken joints*	*six*
600 ml	*brown ale*	*1 pint*
ten	*juniper berries*	*ten*
one	*bouquet garni (page 216)*	*one*
two	*carrots*	*two*
two	*onions*	*two*
110 g	*butter*	*¼ lb*
	salt, pepper	
two 15 ml spoons	*genever (or gin)*	*2 tablesp*
25 g	*flour*	*1 oz*
25 g	*dark brown sugar*	*1 oz*
four 15 ml spoons	*single cream*	*4 tablesp*

Marinate the chicken joints overnight in the ale, with the juniper berries, the bouquet garni and the sliced carrots and onions. The next day pat the chicken dry and lightly brown the pieces in the hot butter. Season well. Warm the genever in a soup ladle, ignite it and pour it over the chicken. When the flames have subsided, sprinkle the flour and sugar over the chicken and stir well. Pour over the marinade, including the juniper berries, herbs and vegetables. Cover the pan, and simmer the chicken for about 45 minutes, or cook it in a moderate oven (180°C, 350°F, mark 4). Just before serving, add the cream and warm it through. Correct the seasoning before serving.

Chicken breasts in sparkling wine

one	*carrot*	*one*
one	*onion*	*one*
110 g	*mushrooms*	*¼ lb*
25 g	*butter*	*1 oz*
300 ml	*dry sparkling wine*	*½ pint*
six	*chicken breasts*	*six*
	(approx. 175 g/6 oz each)	
	salt, pepper	
150 ml	*single cream*	*¼ pint*

Finely chop the vegetables and place them in a shallow oven-proof dish with the butter and wine. Skin and bone the chicken breasts and fold them in half. Lay them on the bed of vegetables and season them well. Cover the dish, and cook it in a moderately slow oven (160°C, 325°F, mark 3) for 45 minutes. Remove the chicken and keep it warm. Cook the sauce over a high heat to reduce it by half. Add the cream and warm it through. Strain the sauce onto the chicken.

Substitute a still dry white wine for the sparkling wine, if you wish.

Poulet à l'orange

Why should duck be the only dish to be served 'à l'orange'? Here is a quickly-made chicken version which tastes all the better using bitter oranges, if they are available.

two	*oranges*	*two*
100 ml	*Grand Marnier or other orange liqueur*	*3 fl oz*
two 15 ml spoons	*wine vinegar*	*2 tablesp*
four 15 ml spoons	*brown sugar*	*4 tablesp*
one 5 ml spoon	*freshly-grated nutmeg*	*1 teasp*
two 5 ml spoons	*fresh basil (or half quantity dried)*	*2 teasp*
one	*clove of garlic*	*one*
six	*chicken joints*	*six*
	flour	
	salt, pepper	
	butter or oil	

Place the peeled and sliced oranges in a pan together with the liqueur, vinegar, sugar, nutmeg, basil and crushed garlic. Cook everything slowly for ten minutes, stirring from time to time.

Pass the chicken joints through seasoned flour and brown them in the hot fat. Add the prepared sauce, cover the pan, and simmer the contents gently, for about 35 minutes, until the chicken is cooked. Baste it with the sauce occasionally during cooking.

Served with a crisp green salad, this looks as good as it tastes.

Chicken with almond sauce

Almonds and chicken make a happy partnership, and the tomatoes colour the sauce a delicate pink which makes the dish very pretty.

2–2.25 kg	*roasting chicken or*	*4–4½ lb*
four–six	*joints*	*four–six*
50 g	*butter*	*2 oz*
two 15 ml spoons	*brandy*	*2 tablesp*
two 15 ml spoons	*flour*	*2 tablesp*
400 g	*tinned tomatoes*	*14 oz*
300 ml	*chicken stock (page 215)*	*½ pint*
150 ml	*dry white wine*	*¼ pint*
150 ml	*single cream*	*¼ pint*
50 g	*ground almonds*	*2 oz*
50 g	*flaked almonds*	*2 oz*

In a heavy saucepan brown the jointed chicken in the melted butter. Warm the brandy in a soup ladle, ignite it and pour it over the chicken. Let the flames subside before removing the chicken.

To make the sauce, stir the flour into the fat remaining in the pan. Sieve the tinned tomatoes into the pan, stir well, and let them simmer for a few minutes. Add the stock and wine, and bring the sauce to the boil before adding the cream and the ground almonds. Season the sauce well.

Return the chicken pieces to the pan, cover it, and simmer it for 30 minutes, or until the chicken is tender. Before serving, scatter the flaked almonds over the chicken.

Arroz con pollo

2–2.25 kg	roasting chicken or	4–4½ lb
four–six	joints	four–six
	flour	
	salt, pepper	
	oil	
two	cloves of garlic	two
110 g	cooked ham	¼ lb
110 g	tinned sweet pimento	¼ lb
one	medium-sized onion	one
one 5 ml spoon	sweet paprika	1 teasp
one	pinch of cayenne pepper	one
225 g	long-grain rice	½ lb
600 ml	chicken stock (page 215)	1 pint
200 ml	dry white wine	7 fl oz
400 g	tinned tomatoes	14 oz
one	strip of lemon peel	one
one 5 ml spoon	sugar	1 teasp

Joint the chicken and pass the pieces through seasoned flour. Brown them in hot oil with the crushed garlic. Remove the chicken and add the chopped ham, pimento and onion. Stir in the paprika and cayenne; add the rice and stir again. Pour on the stock, wine and tomatoes. Add the lemon peel and sugar. Return the chicken to the pan, cover it and cook it in a moderate oven (180°C, 350°F, mark 4) for one hour.

Turkey fillets in cream sauce

700 g (approx.)	turkey fillets	1½ lb (approx.)
	salt, pepper	
50 g	butter	2 oz
one	large onion	one
350 g	tomatoes	¾ lb
150 ml	dry white wine	¼ pint
150 ml	single cream	¼ pint

Season the turkey fillets and cook them in the hot butter over a moderate heat in a covered pan for 25 minutes, turning them from time to time.

Remove the fillets from the pan and keep them warm. Add the finely-chopped onion to the pan and cook it gently until it is soft. Add the skinned, de-seeded and chopped tomatoes to the pan, together with the wine and cream. Cook gently for about five minutes. Return the fillets to the pan and warm them in the sauce.

Celebration turkey (10–12)

This recipe produces a very succulent turkey which is equally good hot or cold, and therefore a useful buffet-party dish.

5 kg (approx.)	turkey	10 lb (approx.)
	salt, pepper	
one	large lemon	one
two 5 ml spoons	grated nutmeg	2 teasp
one 5 ml spoon	ground mace	1 teasp
one	pinch of ground cloves	one
450 g	streaky bacon	1 lb
one	sprig of rosemary	one
four	bay leaves	four
300 ml	dry white wine	½ pint
300 ml	water	½ pint
	chicken fat or butter	

Rinse the turkey inside and out and dry it well. Season the cavity with salt and pepper.

Grate the lemon rind and squeeze the juice. Put the rind in a plastic bag with the spices and rindless bacon rashers. Shake the bag to coat the bacon with the spices. Reserve half the rashers for covering the breast and pack the remainder into the cavity of the bird, together with the rosemary and bay leaves. Truss the bird for roasting. Mix the lemon juice, wine and water in a roasting-tin. Put the turkey in the tin on its side and leave it in a cool place for six hours, turning it from time to time to soak the breasts and sides well.

Take the bird out of the marinade and pat it dry. Brush it with the melted chicken fat or butter. Cover the breast with the reserved bacon rashers. Return the bird to the roasting-tin with the breast uppermost. Cover the whole tin with greased foil, tucking it well down over the sides to seal it. Cook the bird, covered, in a hot oven (220°C, 425°F, mark 7) for about 2½ hours. Remove the foil and the bacon, baste the turkey with the pan juices and return it to the oven for 15 minutes, until it is golden brown. Serve either hot or cold.

Poussins au pays d'Auge

Poulet vallée d'Auge is possibly a more famous version of this dish, and indeed they are really interchangeable.

110 g	butter	¼ lb
six	small poussins (or three large)	six
six	dessert apples	six
100 ml	calvados	3 fl oz
425 ml	dry cider	14 fl oz
	salt, pepper	
100 ml	double cream	3 fl oz

Reserve a quarter of the butter and melt the rest in a large, flame-proof casserole. Lightly brown the poussins and the peeled and cored apples (left whole). Warm the calvados in a soup ladle, ignite it and pour it over the poussins. When the flames have died down, add the cider to the pan. Season well, cover the pan, and simmer the poussins gently, turning them from time to time. Take care that the apples don't overcook – they should keep their shape. When they begin to soften, remove them from the pan and keep them warm. Continue to cook the poussins until they are ready, which should take about 40 minutes. Remove them from the pan and keep them warm with the apples.

Add the cream and reduce the sauce to thicken it a little. Add the reserved butter and whisk it in vigorously. Pour the sauce over the poussins and apples and serve them immediately.

Turkey fillets with various sauces

Turkey fillets, poached or baked and served with a suitable sauce, make a quick but impressive dish. Add hot French bread and a tossed salad to complete the meal.

700 g (approx.)	turkey fillets	1½ lb (approx.)
	salt, pepper	
300 ml	chicken stock (page 215) or	½ pint
25 g	butter	1 oz

Season the turkey fillets and place them in a shallow oven-proof dish. Add either the stock or the butter. Cover the dish and cook the fillets in a moderate oven (180°C, 350°F, mark 4) for about 25 minutes until the fillets are tender.

While the turkey is cooking, make one of the following: cherry sauce (page 183); wine sauce (pages 184 and 186); sauce diable (page 182); sherry cream sauce (page 188).

Put the fillets on a serving dish. Coat with a little of the prepared sauce and serve the rest separately.

Duck with orange

Perhaps this is the most popular of all ways of cooking duck, and rightly so in my opinion. The sharpness of the oranges seems to cut the fattiness of duck, especially if you can use Sevilles for the juice (I keep a few in my freezer for recipes like this).

2.5 kg (approx.)	*duck with giblets*	*5 lb (approx.)*
	salt, pepper	
three 15 ml spoons	*sugar*	*3 tablesp*
100 ml	*water*	*3 fl oz*
	butter	
one	*medium-sized onion*	*one*
one	*stick of celery*	*one*
one	*small carrot*	*one*
two 5 ml spoons	*fresh thyme*	*2 teasp*
	(or half quantity dried)	
one	*bay leaf*	*one*
150 ml	*dry white wine*	*¼ pint*
300 ml	*water*	*½ pint*
one 15 ml spoon	*cornflour*	*1 tablesp*
five	*oranges*	*five*
two 15 ml spoons	*redcurrant jelly*	*2 tablesp*
three 15 ml spoons	*Grand Marnier*	*3 tablesp*
	watercress	

Remove the giblets and rinse the duck inside and out. Pat it dry and prick it all over. Season well and place the duck on a rack in a roasting-tin. Cook it in a hot oven (220°C, 425°F, mark 7) for ten minutes, reduce the heat to 180°C (350°F, mark 4) and cook it for a further 1½ hours.

While the duck is cooking, make the sauce. Cook the sugar with the 100 ml (3 fl oz) water until it begins to caramelise. Reserve this for later use.

Wash the giblets and pat them dry. Toss them in the hot butter. Add the finely-chopped onion, celery and carrot, along with the thyme, bay leaf, salt and pepper. Stir well and pour on the wine and water. Bring the mixture to the boil and simmer the sauce for half an hour. Strain it onto the caramel and cook for five minutes. Mix the cornflour with a little water and add it to the sauce. Cook until it has thickened, stirring all the time. Adjust the seasoning.

Add the juice of three of the oranges, the redcurrant jelly and the Grand Marnier. Bring the sauce to the boil, reduce the heat, and keep it warm until it is needed. Peel the remaining two oranges (not Sevilles, this time) and cut them into very thin slices. When the duck is ready, remove it from the oven and put it on a serving platter. Garnish it with the slices of orange. Pour over a little of the sauce and serve the rest separately. Garnish with watercress.

You can make a pretty garnish by cutting very thin strips of orange peel (without any pith) and blanching them in boiling water for three minutes. Scatter the peel over the duck before serving.

Duck with cherries

The cherry sauce referred to in this recipe is equally suitable for turkey or chicken.

Follow the instructions for roasting a whole duck in the previous recipe, duck with orange. If you prefer to use individual pieces of duck, season them well and roast them in a hot oven (220°C, 425°F, mark 7) for ten minutes and then reduce the heat to 180°C (350°F, mark 4) and cook for a further hour.

Make the cherry sauce (page 183) and serve it with the cooked duck.

Duck with green peppercorn sauce

four–six	pieces of duck	four–six
	salt, pepper	
150 ml	dry white wine	¼ pint
150 ml	duck or chicken stock (page 215)	¼ pint
50 ml	brandy	2 fl oz
two 15 ml spoons	green peppercorns	2 tablesp
two 5 ml spoons	cornflour	2 teasp

Place the pieces of duck in a roasting-tin. Season them well, and add the wine and stock. Cook the duck, uncovered, in a moderate oven (180°C, 350°F, mark 4) for 1¼ hours. Remove the duck and return it to the oven on a clean oven-dish, increasing the heat to 220° (425°F, mark 7) for 15 minutes.

To make the sauce, skim off the fat from the liquid in the roasting-tin. Add the brandy and green peppercorns. Mix the cornflour with a little cold water and add it to the sauce. Stir well, and cook until it has thickened. Remove the duck from the oven and put it on a serving dish. Pour over a little sauce and serve the rest separately.

Offal

In the interests of research I looked up a dictionary definition of 'offal' and found it to be a most unappetising collection of words . . . 'refuse, waste stuff, scraps, garbage'. Not likely to stimulate the gastric juices, you might think. The American 'variety meats' and the French 'abats' are scarcely more encouraging.

All this is rather sad when you think how very delicious – and indeed nutritious – these meats are. Liver features prominently in many slimming diets, for its high protein and low fat content, though smothering it in onions and swamping it in wine or beer might not be quite what the dieticians have in mind.

I confess to a youthful dislike of kidneys until I tried cooking them in wine, and realised what I had been missing. The same applies to many other branches of this family of meats, all of which are enhanced by a drop of wine or spirits.

Perhaps after all the American 'variety meats' is the best description of this disparate collection, because variety is most certainly what you will add to your menu by offering offal.

Oxtail in beer

Sadly, oxtail isn't the inexpensive cut it was in my youth, but it does make a lovely hearty winter meal – the more so with a rich and comforting gravy of beer.

225 g	*dried haricot beans*	*½ lb*
350 g	*onions*	*¾ lb*
	oil	
1.75 kg (approx.)	*jointed oxtail*	*3½ lb (approx.)*
	flour	
	salt, pepper	
three	*sticks of celery*	*three*
one	*bouquet garni (page 216)*	*one*
600 ml	*beef stock (page 214)*	*1 pint*
300 ml	*brown ale*	*½ pint*

This is a two-day event as the beans need to be soaked overnight and the oxtail is also cooked the day before to allow the fat to be removed when it is cool.

Soak the beans overnight. In a heavy, flame-proof casserole, soften the sliced onions in hot oil. Pass the pieces of oxtail through seasoned flour and brown them in the oil. Add the chopped celery, bouquet garni and stock. Bring everything to the boil, cover the pan, and simmer it for one hour. Leave the oxtail to cool overnight. The next day skim off the fat.

Cook the haricots, separately, very slowly for two hours (or for about ten minutes in a pressure-cooker). Don't let them become too soft as they will be further cooked in the casserole.

Pour the ale over the oxtail, cover the casserole, and cook it over low heat or in a low oven (160°C, 325°F, mark 3) for 1½ hours. Add the beans and cook the oxtail for a further 1½ hours. Check the liquid and add more stock if necessary.

Braised oxtail

1.75 kg (approx.)	*jointed oxtail*	*3½ lb (approx.)*
	flour	
	salt, pepper	
	oil	
225 g	*onions*	*½ lb*
225 g	*carrots*	*½ lb*
three	*sticks of celery*	*three*
two	*leeks*	*two*
450 ml	*red wine*	*¾ pint*
two 15 ml spoons	*tomato puree*	*2 tablesp*
one	*bouquet garni (page 216)*	*one*

It is best to cook the oxtail the day before it is required to allow the fat to be removed when it is cool.

Cover the oxtail with water and bring it to the boil. Simmer the contents, covered, for one hour. Remove the oxtail and reserve 450 ml (¾ pint) of the liquid. Pat the pieces dry and pass them through seasoned flour. In a heavy flame-proof casserole brown them in hot oil. Add the chopped vegetables to the casserole and cook them for five minutes. Add the wine, tomato puree, bouquet garni and reserved stock. Season well, and stir everything together thoroughly. Cover the casserole, and cook it in a moderately slow oven (160°C, 325°F, mark 3) for 2½ hours. Leave the oxtail to cool overnight, and skim off the fat.

Check the liquid and if necessary add a little more stock and wine before cooking the casserole for a further hour.

Rognons flambés

Kidneys tend to look rather a meagre dish on their own but are in fact quite filling. A smaller quantity of this recipe would make an excellent first course. The 'B and B' gives a particularly delicious flavour.

12–14	lambs' kidneys	12–14
	butter	
350 g	button mushrooms	3/4 lb
	salt, pepper	
four 15 ml spoons	Bénédictine and Brandy	4 tablesp

Slice the kidneys, removing the core and any fat. Cook them, starting with the cut side down, in hot butter for 3–5 minutes over a high heat. Remove them while you cook the sliced mushrooms. Return the kidneys to the pan, season them well and keep them warm over a very low heat.

Warm the liqueur in a soup ladle, ignite it and pour it over the contents of the pan. When the flames subside, serve the kidneys – on a bed of rice, if you wish.

Chicken livers with vermouth

Any quickly-made dish is a useful part of a cook's repertoire and chicken livers fill the bill nicely.

one	large onion	one
	oil	
75 g	bacon	3 oz
one	large clove of garlic	one
700 g	chicken livers	1½ lb
one 5 ml spoon	fresh basil	1 teasp
	(or half quantity dried)	
	salt, pepper	
two 5 ml spoons	tomato puree	2 teasp
100 ml	dry vermouth	3 fl oz

Soften the chopped onion in the oil. Add the chopped bacon and crushed garlic and cook for a minute. Remove any green bile from the livers before adding them to the pan. Cook them for five minutes, turning them gently. Add the basil, salt and pepper, tomato puree and vermouth. Stir the contents of the pan, cover it and simmer for ten minutes.

Serve with buttered noodles or rice.

Kidneys with vermouth

This is the sort of dish you could put together at very short notice and still impress your guests considerably. The vermouth can be either sweet or dry.

12–14	*lambs' kidneys*	*12–14*
one 15 ml spoon	*flour*	*1 tablesp*
	butter	
350 g	*mushrooms*	*¾ lb*
	salt, pepper	
150 ml	*white vermouth*	*¼ pint*
100 ml	*water*	*3 fl oz*
three 15 ml spoons	*single cream*	*3 tablesp*
	chopped parsley	

Cut the kidneys in half, remove the core and slice them through again. Pass the kidneys through the flour and brown them in hot butter. Add the sliced mushrooms and cook everything for three minutes, stirring constantly. Season with salt and pepper and turn the contents of the pan into an oven-dish. Pour on the vermouth and water.

Cover the dish and cook it in a slow oven (160°C, 325°F, mark 3) for 20 minutes, or over a low heat on top of the stove. Check the seasoning. Pour on the cream, sprinkle over the parsley and stir through.

Serve the kidneys on a bed of rice.

Chicken livers with crisp vegetables

I devised this recipe for a calorie-controlled diet in which wine was to be an essential ingredient. To my delight I discovered that the addition of a modest amount of wine or dry sherry need not increase the calories beyond acceptable limits. The calorie count, for those who are interested, works out at approximately 225 per portion (based on the recipe feeding six people).

three	*sticks of celery*	*three*
two	*medium-sized onions*	*two*
175 g	*green pepper*	*6 oz*
350 g	*button mushrooms*	*3/4 lb*
350 g	*tinned tomatoes*	*3/4 lb*
half 5 ml spoon	*grated nutmeg*	*1/2 teasp*
one and a half 15 ml spoons	*tomato puree*	*1 1/2 tablesp*
	salt, pepper	
700 g	*chicken livers*	*1 1/2 lb*
100 ml	*dry sherry*	*3 fl oz*

Chop all the raw vegetables finely and put them into a pan with the tinned tomatoes, nutmeg, tomato puree, salt and pepper. Cover the pan and simmer the contents for a few minutes.

Meanwhile, wash the livers and pat them dry. Take care to remove any green bile. Season them well, and grill them for five minutes, or until they are lightly browned but still pink inside. Add the grilled livers to the vegetables, together with the sherry. Cook for a further five minutes, stirring from time to time. The vegetables should still be crisp when the livers are cooked.

Serve the dish on bean-sprouts or, for non-slimmers, rice. Add a dash of soy sauce for an even more Oriental slant.

Fegato alla veneziana

Unlike most children, I always loved liver, and never more so than when fried with masses of onions. Now I add a little wine and an Italian name and it's still a favourite meal. Ideally you should use calf's liver and have it very thinly sliced.

450 g	onions	1 lb
	oil, butter	
700 g	liver	1½ lb
	salt, pepper	
200 ml	dry white wine	7 fl oz
	chopped parsley	

Cook the thinly-sliced onions in the hot oil and a little butter in a heavy frying-pan. When they are soft and golden, remove them from the pan and keep them warm while you cook the liver. Depending on the thickness, you should need to cook it for only a few minutes on each side and it should be a little pink in the centre. Season it well. Return the onions to the pan. Add the wine and simmer it for a few minutes. Serve immediately, sprinkled with chopped parsley.

Liver with beer

Calf's liver is nicest, but ox or lamb's liver works perfectly well in this dish.

450 g	onions	1 lb
	oil, butter	
700 g	liver	1½ lb
	flour	
	salt, pepper	
300 ml	brown ale	½ pint

Slice the onions and soften them in the oil and butter in a heavy frying-pan. Pass the thinly-sliced liver through well-seasoned flour. Remove the onions from the pan and keep them warm. Add the liver to the pan and sauté it for a few minutes on each side. It should be a little pink in the centre. Return the onions to the pan. Add the ale and stir it round well to release any sediment on the bottom of the pan. Leave the contents to cook over a gentle heat for about five minutes. Serve the dish with creamed potatoes to mop up the rich gravy.

Tongue with madeira sauce

Hot tongue is an altogether different matter from the cold pressed tongue you buy sliced and ready to serve. Not everyone can face cooking a whole tongue, but it is such a delicacy that it is well worth a moment's discomfort. For the squeamish, it is in any case served in slices so that its origins are veiled in madeira sauce, if not obscurity.

1.5–1.75 kg	*salted (pickled) ox tongue*	*3–3½ lb*
one	*onion*	*one*
one	*carrot*	*one*
one	*stick of celery*	*one*
one	*leek*	*one*
one 15 ml spoon	*mixed pickling spice*	*1 tablesp*
	madeira sauce (page 183)	

If you aren't sure how well pickled the tongue is, you may care to soak it overnight to remove any excess salt. Or you can bring it to the boil in plain water before starting to cook it. A good butcher will have left it in brine for the correct time and you can taste how salty it is by touching it and licking your finger. Some supermarket chains sell pickled tongue and I have generally found them to be satisfactory.

Wash the tongue and place it in a large pan together with the chopped vegetables and the pickling spice. Bring the water to the boil, cover, and simmer the tongue for about 2½ hours, or until it is very tender. I prefer to pressure-cook it which cuts down the time to one hour.

Meanwhile make the madeira sauce.

When the tongue is cooked, let it cool for half an hour or so in the pan before carefully removing the skin and any bits of gristle. Carve the tongue into thin slices using a very sharp knife. Place the slices in a shallow, flame-proof dish and pour over the sauce. Warm it through gently.

Serve with creamed potatoes and buttered cabbage.

This is obviously a basic recipe for preparing tongue and you could serve it with another sauce if preferred: port (page 183), lyonnaise (page 186), tomato (page 187) . . .

Sweetbread terrine

This interesting way of preparing sweetbreads is as much a mousse as a terrine. It looks rather complicated but if you have a liquidiser or a food processor you can make short work of it. There are three different stages, the choux pastry, the liquidised ingredients and the diced ingredients.

110 g	*butter*	*¼ lb*
300 ml	*milk*	*½ pint*
125 g	*flour*	*4½ oz*
four	*egg yolks*	*four*
three 15 ml spoons	*chopped shallots*	*3 tablesp*
	butter	
280 g	*prepared sweetbreads (page 129)*	*10 oz*
280 g	*cooked ham*	*10 oz*
three 15 ml spoons	*chopped parsley*	*3 tablesp*
four	*egg whites*	*four*
	salt, pepper	
300 ml	*single cream*	*½ pint*
175 g	*prepared sweetbreads (page 129)*	*6 oz*
110 g	*mushrooms*	*¼ lb*
	butter	
one	*pinch of grated nutmeg*	*one*
100 ml	*brandy*	*3 fl oz*

First make the choux pastry by melting the butter with the milk in a saucepan and quickly beating in the flour until it is smooth and forms a ball. Add the egg yolks one at a time, beating each one in well. Leave the mixture in the pan until it is required.

Soften the chopped shallots in the hot butter and liquidise or process them with the 280 g (10 oz) sweetbreads, the ham, parsley, choux pastry, egg whites, salt, pepper and cream. You may have to do this in several batches, depending on the size of your machine. Blend everything well and turn the mixed ingredients into a bowl.

Dice the remaining sweetbreads and mushrooms and toss them in a little melted butter. Add the nutmeg. Warm the brandy in a soup ladle, ignite it and pour it over the diced sweetbreads. Stir the mixture until the flames subside. Fold this diced mixture gently into the liquidised ingredients.

Butter a terrine and line it with foil. Turn the combined mixtures into the terrine and cook it in a moderate oven (180°C, 350°F, mark 4) for 1¼ hours. Unmould the terrine and serve it hot, with a port or madeira sauce if you wish (page 183). If you prefer to serve it from the dish, there is no need to line it with foil. For a 'nouvelle cuisine' effect, line the terrine carefully with blanched lettuce leaves or spinach.

Sweetbreads with calvados

700 g	*sweetbreads*	*1½ lb*
	vinegar	
six	*dessert apples*	*six*
50 g	*butter*	*2 oz*
	salt, pepper	
two 15 ml spoons	*calvados*	*2 tablesp*
six 15 ml spoons	*single cream*	*6 tablesp*

Soak the sweetbreads for several hours in a bowl of water with a spoonful of vinegar added. Change the water and vinegar after two hours and leave the sweetbreads to soak for a further two hours. This helps to soften the membrane round the sweetbreads so that you can remove it carefully. Pat the sweetbreads dry.

Peel and core the apples and cook them in half the butter until they are just beginning to soften. Remove them and keep them warm. Add the rest of the butter to the pan and cook the sweetbreads over a very low heat for 30 minutes, turning them from time to time. Season with the salt and pepper. Heat the calvados in a soup ladle, ignite it and pour it over the sweetbreads. When the flames subside, add the cream and stir it to warm it through.

Serve the sweetbreads with the cooked apples and the creamy sauce.

Game

Game used to be rather esoteric – unless you knew someone on the huntin', shootin' and fishin' scene you might well not come across pheasant or rabbit, wood pigeon or venison. All these delicacies, and many more, are now becoming quite readily available in larger supermarkets and freezer shops. Our horizons are being widened and I for one welcome it as I am frequently heard sighing in the butcher's that it would be nice if someone were to invent a new variety of meat.

The connection between game and alcohol is an important one since many recipes require a marinade of wine or beer. This may be because the meat tends to be rather dry, but perhaps it is also to disguise any excessively high flavour acquired in the hanging process.

Lapin au cidre

You may care to use the boned rabbit which is available in some supermarkets or freezer shops since it usually represents better value than either pieces or the whole rabbit. The flavour is 'tamer' than that of fresh, free-range rabbit.

1 kg	*boned rabbit*	*2 lb*
	(or equivalent of whole rabbit)	
	oil	
450 g	*onions*	*1 lb*
four	*shallots*	*four*
two	*cloves of garlic*	*two*
one 15 ml spoon	*flour*	*1 tablesp*
600 ml	*dry cider*	*1 pint*
one	*clove*	*one*
	salt, pepper	

If you are using fresh, whole rabbit, cut it into pieces. Brown the rabbit pieces in oil in a heavy saucepan. Remove them and add the chopped onions, peeled shallots and crushed garlic. Stir them round and leave them to colour a little before returning the rabbit to the pan. Add the flour, stirring it in well, the cider and the clove. Season everything thoroughly. Cover the pan, and simmer it for 45 minutes for boned rabbit and one hour for joints with the bone in.

Turnips are a traditional accompaniment to rabbit in France: add 1 kg (2 lb) of diced, white turnips to the casserole for the last 15 minutes of cooking.

Casserole of hare

Hare is very meaty meat, usually marinated before cooking. In this Italian recipe you may be surprised at the addition of a small amount of chocolate. This is not uncommon in game cookery from the Mediterranean, and in Mexico a chilli-and-chocolate sauce (mole) makes even turkey taste like exotic game. It gives extra richness to the sauce but is not sufficient to make you think you are eating a chocolate Easter bunny.

one	*hare (approx. 2.5 kg/5 lb)*	*one*
one	*large onion*	*one*
two	*carrots*	*two*
two	*cloves of garlic*	*two*
	parsley stalks	
eight 15 ml spoons	*olive oil*	*8 tablesp*
600 ml	*full-bodied red wine*	*1 pint*
	salt, pepper	
	flour	
300 ml	*beef stock (page 214)*	*½ pint*
15 g	*plain chocolate*	*½ oz*
three	*cloves*	*three*

Ask the butcher to joint the hare into six or eight pieces. Place the pieces in a large pottery or enamelled dish. Add the sliced onion and carrots, the crushed garlic, the parsley stalks, half the oil and half the wine. Season the mixture and turn the hare in it. Leave it to marinate for 24 hours, turning it from time to time.

Remove the hare from the marinade, pat it dry and pass the pieces through seasoned flour. In a heavy flame-proof casserole, brown them in the remaining oil. Strain the marinade onto the hare, add the rest of the wine, the stock, the grated chocolate, the cloves and more salt and pepper. Bring the mixture to the boil, and then reduce the heat, cover the casserole, and simmer it for about 1½ hours. Thicken the sauce by reduction (page 218) if necessary.

Rabbit with beer

1 kg	boned rabbit	2 lb
	(or equivalent of whole rabbit)	
	oil	
225 g	onions	½ lb
	salt, pepper	
ten	juniper berries	ten
one	clove of garlic	one
one	bouquet garni (page 216)	one
110 g	mushrooms	¼ lb
600 ml	light ale	1 pint
one	lemon	one

If you are using fresh, whole rabbit, cut it into pieces. Brown the rabbit pieces in oil in a heavy saucepan. Add the sliced onions and brown them. Stir in the salt and pepper, crushed juniper berries, crushed garlic and the bouquet garni.

Add the ale and the juice of the lemon. Cover the pan and simmer it for 45 minutes for boned rabbit and one hour for joints with the bone in, adding the sliced mushrooms for the last 10–15 minutes. Thicken the sauce with beurre manié (page 216) if necessary.

Noisettes of venison

six	noisettes of venison	six
300 ml	dry white wine	½ pint
six	juniper berries	six
one	bouquet garni (page 216)	one
one	small carrot	one
one	small onion	one
	salt, pepper	
25 g	butter	1 oz
two 15 ml spoons	brandy	2 tablesp
four 15 ml spoons	double cream	4 tablesp
two 15 ml spoons	redcurrant jelly	2 tablesp

Marinate the venison for 24 hours in the wine, with the crushed juniper berries, the bouquet garni, the finely-chopped carrot and onion, and salt and pepper.

Remove the venison from the marinade and pat it dry. Fry the noisettes in hot butter for about five minutes on each side, depending on the thickness. Remove them from the pan and keep them warm while you make the sauce.

Strain the marinade into the pan and reduce it by half over a high heat. Heat the brandy in a soup ladle, ignite it, and pour it into the pan. When the flames subside, stir in the cream and the redcurrant jelly. Stir the sauce until the jelly has dissolved. Correct the seasoning. Spoon the sauce over the venison and serve it immediately.

If you cannot get noisettes of venison you can use stewing venison, in very thin strips.

Venison stew

Although it is rather a luxury, venison is a most delicious meat and well worth the occasional extravagance. Ask how long it has been hung when you buy it since this affects the tenderness as well as the 'height'.

1.25–1.5 kg	*stewing venison*	*2½–3 lb*
110 g	*bacon*	*¼ lb*
	oil	
one	*large clove of garlic*	*one*
225 g	*carrots*	*½ lb*
two	*sticks of celery*	*two*
450 ml	*full-bodied red wine*	*¾ pint*
600 ml	*beef stock (page 214)*	*1 pint*
one	*bouquet garni (page 216)*	*one*
	salt, pepper	
225 g	*button mushrooms*	*½ lb*
40 g	*butter*	*1½ oz*
40 g	*flour*	*1½ oz*
150 ml	*sour cream*	*¼ pint*
	redcurrant jelly	

Cut the venison into 5-cm (2-inch) cubes. Fry the chopped bacon in a little oil. Add the crushed garlic and the venison, a little at a time, and brown it well. Remove the meat to a casserole. Add the chopped vegetables, wine, stock, bouquet garni, salt and plenty of freshly-ground pepper. Cover the casserole, and cook it in a moderately slow oven (160°C, 325°F, mark 3) for one hour. Add the sliced mushrooms and cook the casserole for a further 30 minutes.

Make a roux (page 217) with the butter and flour. When the venison is ready, strain the liquid from it onto the roux and stir it over a gentle heat to make a smooth sauce. Cook it for three minutes. Stir in the sour cream and warm it through. Pour the sauce over the venison and serve it with the redcurrant jelly.

Ardèche guinea-fowl

Guinea-fowl can make a very pleasant change from chicken and is now becoming easier to obtain in large supermarkets as well as from specialist butchers. This recipe concentrates on the accompaniments to the bird and, though it seems rather elaborate, it can be put together surprisingly quickly with quite impressive results.

There is a high concentration of meat on guinea-fowl and you should find that a seemingly quite small bird will be sufficient for four people.

1.5 kg (approx.)	*guinea-fowl*	*3 lb (approx.)*
	butter	
	salt, pepper	
200 ml	*white wine*	*7 fl oz*
200 ml	*chicken stock (page 215)*	*7 fl oz*
six	*small pears*	*six*
100 ml	*red wine*	*3 fl oz*
450 g	*chestnuts*	*1 lb*
one	*small white cabbage*	*one*

In a heavy pan brown the guinea-fowl on all sides in hot butter. Season it well. Pour over half the white wine and half the stock. Cover the pan and cook it over a low heat for about 45 minutes, until the guinea-fowl is tender. While it is cooking, prepare the accompaniments.

Peel the pears, leaving them whole. Poach them very gently in the red wine, which will all be absorbed when the pears are soft. Keep them warm.

Slit the chestnuts and cover them with water. Bring them to the boil, cook them for five minutes, and peel them, removing the inner skin. Try to keep them whole. Put them into a pan with the rest of the white wine and stock and cook them, covered, until they are tender, by which time they will have absorbed all the liquid. Keep an eye on them and add a little more wine and water if necessary. Shred the cabbage finely and cook it in a little butter, just until it is *al dente*.

When the guinea-fowl is ready, cut it into four portions and place it on a bed of the cooked cabbage, surrounded by the chestnuts and pears. Serve the gravy separately.

Normandy pheasant

This close cousin of poussins au pays d'Auge (page 116) is a most tasty way to prepare pheasant, which can be rather dry if not carefully cooked. Quantities are difficult with pheasant. Two pheasants should serve five quite well, although the helpings might not look very generous. The meat is quite rich, particularly cooked in this way. Plain vegetables are best, in order not to detract from the creamy sauce.

two	*large pheasants*	*two*
50 g	*butter*	*2 oz*
	salt, pepper	
450 g	*crisp dessert apples*	*1 lb*
150 ml	*calvados*	*¼ pint*
200 ml	*single cream*	*7 fl oz*

Wash the pheasants inside and out, pat them dry, and pick out stray pin-feathers with tweezers.

In a heavy flame-proof casserole, brown the pheasants in hot butter and season them well. Remove them and add the peeled, cored and thinly-sliced apples to the casserole. Cook them until they begin to soften.

Place the pheasants on top of the apples, breasts downwards or sideways if possible. Warm the calvados in a soup ladle, ignite it and pour it over the pheasants. When the flames subside, cover the casserole and cook it in a moderate oven (180°C, 350°F, mark 4) for one hour. Add the cream and return the casserole to the oven for a further 30 minutes, or more, until the pheasants are cooked.

Carve the pheasants and serve them with the sauce. The apples will almost have melted away and the sauce should be thick and creamy.

Wood pigeons in red wine

When wood pigeons first appeared (commercially, that is) a few years ago, I didn't know what to do with them. I cooked them in the same way as coq au vin (page 110), and since that met with great approval, I've continued to do so. You might care to warn your guests to look out for odd pieces of shot.

six	*wood pigeons*	*six*
	seasoned flour	
	butter	
225 g	*button onions*	*½ lb*
two	*cloves of garlic*	*two*
225 g	*streaky bacon*	*½ lb*
two 5 ml spoons	*fresh thyme*	*2 teasp*
	(or half quantity dried)	
two 5 ml spoons	*fresh marjoram*	*2 teasp*
	(or half quantity dried)	
450 ml	*full-bodied red wine*	*¾ pint*
150 ml	*chicken stock (page 215)*	*¼ pint*
350 g	*button mushrooms*	*¾ lb*
	salt, pepper	

Wash the wood pigeons well as they tend to have a lot of blood on them. Pat them dry and pass them through seasoned flour. In a heavy flame-proof casserole brown the pigeons in hot butter. Add the peeled onions, the crushed garlic, the chopped bacon and the herbs. Stir everything together before adding the wine and stock. Bring the liquid to the boil and cover the casserole. Cook it in a slow oven (150°C, 300°F, mark 2) for 2½ hours. Add the whole mushrooms and return the casserole to the oven for a further 30 minutes. Check the seasoning.

If you prefer to cook this one day and re-heat it the next, do not add the mushrooms until half an hour before you are going to serve the dish.

Wood pigeons in beer

six	*wood pigeons*	*six*
600 ml	*dark ale*	*1 pint*
one	*onion*	*one*
one	*carrot*	*one*
one	*bouquet garni (page 216)*	*one*
	salt, pepper	
700 g	*chestnuts*	*1½ lb*
	flour	
	oil	
	butter	
225 g	*button onions*	*½ lb*
300 ml	*chicken stock (page 215)*	*½ pint*

Wash the wood pigeons well and pat them dry.

Marinate the pigeons overnight in the ale, along with the sliced onion and carrot, the bouquet garni, salt and pepper. Slit the chestnuts and cook them in boiling water for ten minutes. Drain and peel them, keeping them whole if possible.

Remove the pigeons from the marinade, pat them dry and pass them through flour. In a heavy casserole brown them in a little oil and butter. Add the peeled button onions and cook them until they are golden. Strain the marinade onto the pigeons. Add the peeled chestnuts and half the stock. Put a piece of foil over the pigeons. Cover the casserole and cook it in a slow oven (150°C, 300°F, mark 2) for two hours. Check the liquid from time to time, and add a little more stock if necessary.

Sweets

Liqueurs really find their cookery niche amongst the puddings and pies, creams and confections. Not that wine and cider fail to put in an appearance here. The nearest I have got to using beer in sweets is in a batter and in a syllabub.

To me the appeal of cooking with liqueurs is that it is easy to interchange them and experiment using any number of different flavours. This needn't be as expensive an exercise as you may think because few of the recipes require more than the equivalent of two miniature bottles of liqueur and so, for a relatively small outlay, you can try some of the more esoteric creations which you may hesitate to purchase by the whole bottle. It is also an excellent way of using up those strange-looking concoctions we are all tempted to buy when abroad – the local liqueur of garish colour (and often unspeakable flavour).

A guide to the main liqueurs used here will be found in the table of drinks at the beginning of the book (page 15).

Soufflés

I've never subscribed to the mystique which invariably surrounds the making and serving of soufflés. It must be a hoax perpetrated by the restaurant trade to make us think they are creating something magical in the kitchen. When you realise how easy it is, perhaps you'll agree.

Of course you do need to be sure your 'audience' is ready and waiting since, to the best of my knowledge, no one has yet invented an undeflatable soufflé. Some people are put off making a soufflé because of all that fuss and bother about making a collar around the edge of the dish. If you have a large enough dish this is quite unnecessary. Any straight-sided dish will do – even a cake tin makes a perfectly adequate container.

There are many versions of soufflés but here are just two, on which you can ring whatever changes you like. The first is a simple soufflé requiring only eggs, sugar and your chosen liqueur. It is very light and takes only minutes to prepare. The second, more classic and robust, is based on a white sauce and it can be prepared up to four hours in advance.

Almost any liqueur can be used. Those most frequently found on restaurant menus are probably the orange-based Grand Marnier, Bénédictine and Cointreau, but that need not prevent you from using whatever you prefer. I have used just about every liqueur I could lay my hands on, and never had the thumbs down. Whisky liqueur and 'B and B' are particularly successful, as are other orange liqueurs.

I don't think a soufflé needs any enhancement but possible embellishments to a straightforward soufflé mixture include:
1) sponge cakes or boudoir biscuits, soaked in the liqueur which you are using in the soufflé, cut into small pieces, and added to the soufflé mixture before cooking.
2) finely-chopped candied fruits, soaked in the chosen liqueur, and added to the mixture before cooking (soufflé Rothschild).

Soufflé au liqueur I

This mixture is really enough for four good helpings. If you want more, make half as much again and use two dishes.

	butter	
six	*eggs*	*six*
225 g	*caster sugar*	*½ lb*
four 15 ml spoons	*liqueur*	*4 tablesp*
one	*pinch of cream of tartar*	*one*
one 15 ml spoon	*icing sugar*	*1 tablesp*

Lightly butter one large (2-litre/3½ pints) or two small (one-litre/1¾ pints) soufflé dishes and sprinkle a little caster sugar round the sides. Tip out any surplus. Pre-heat the oven to 160°C (325°F, mark 3).

Separate the eggs, putting the yolks with the caster sugar. If you have an electric beater, beat the yolks and sugar for five minutes at top speed until they are thick and creamy. If you have to beat them by hand it will obviously take rather longer. When the yolks are adequately beaten, stir in the liqueur.

In a second bowl whisk the whites with the cream of tartar until they are very stiff. Take a spoonful and very gently stir it into the yolk mixture to lighten it a little. Fold in the remaining whites. Turn the mixture into the prepared soufflé dish(es). Cook in the oven for 30 minutes for the large soufflé (20 minutes for the two smaller ones). Just before serving, sprinkle the icing sugar on top.

You may find that while the top is quite well browned, there is some runny mixture in the centre of the soufflé. This is inevitable if the outside is not to be overcooked, and the soufflé in fact firms up a little as you are serving it.

Soufflé au liqueur II

50 g	*unsalted butter*	*2 oz*
50 g	*flour*	*2 oz*
450 ml	*milk*	*¾ pint*
two 15 ml spoons	*caster sugar*	*2 tablesp*
six	*eggs*	*six*
five 15 ml spoons	*liqueur*	*5 tablesp*
one 15 ml spoon	*icing sugar*	*1 tablesp*

Butter a large (2-litre/3½-pints) soufflé dish and sprinkle a little sugar round the sides. Tip out any surplus. Pre-heat the oven to 160°C (325°F, mark 3).

In a heavy pan, melt the butter and stir in the flour thoroughly. Off the heat, add the milk gradually, stirring constantly until the sauce is smooth. Return the pan to the heat. Add the caster sugar and stir until the sauce has thickened. Cook it gently for five minutes. Remove the pan from the heat. Separate the eggs and stir the yolks into the sauce quickly. Add the liqueur. Beat the whites until they are very stiff. Scoop a spoonful of the whites and stir them very gently into the yolk mixture. Carefully fold in the rest of the whites, blending them in lightly but well.

Turn the soufflé mixture into the prepared dish and cook it in the oven for 40 minutes. Carefully open the oven door and test the soufflé with a knife or a skewer, as you would a cake. If it comes out clean the soufflé is done; otherwise give it a few minutes more. Sprinkle the icing sugar on top.

If you want to prepare the soufflé in advance, refrigerate it in its dish for up to four hours before cooking it for 50 minutes (ten minutes' additional time).

Pies

Whether you prefer to call them pies or tarts, or possibly even flans, there are many ways of filling a pastry case. Crème pâtissière, gently laced with a little liqueur, and with some fruit on top, makes a quite spectacular sweet which would cost a tidy sum in a French pâtisserie. The art is as much in the presentation as in the cooking, and I find that a 'tarte maison' of whatever variety invariably impresses my guests more than many a richer and more complicated sweet.

Creams and jellies also make delicious fillings. Pastry can be replaced in many cases by a biscuit crust.

Cider cream flan

700 g	cooking apples	1½ lb
two 15 ml spoons	sugar	2 tablesp
50 ml	water	2 fl oz
175 g	walnuts	6 oz
three 15 ml spoons	brown sugar	3 tablesp
25 g	butter	1 oz
225 ml	double cream	8 fl oz
100 ml	sweet cider	3 fl oz
one 15 ml spoon	caster sugar	1 tablesp

Make a thick apple sauce with the apples, sugar and water. If there is a lot of liquid in the apples when they are cooked, continue cooking until it has reduced. Puree the sauce.

While the apples are cooking, make the nut crust: liquidise or process the nuts, brown sugar and butter to a coarse paste. Pat the mixture into a well-greased pie tin (about 20 cm/8 inches). Bake the crust in a hot oven (200°C, 400°F, mark 6) for five minutes only. Turn the apple puree into the nut crust and leave it to cool.

Just before serving, whip the cream, the cider and the caster sugar together to make a syllabub. Spoon this mixture over the pie and serve it immediately.

If you wish, use a baked shortcrust flan case (page 210) instead of the nut crust.

Tarte aux pommes

1 kg	cooking apples	2 lb
25 g	butter	1 oz
75 g	sugar	3 oz
half	cinnamon stick	half
	grated lemon rind	
125 ml	white wine	4 fl oz
three	red dessert apples	three
one 15 ml spoon	sugar	1 tablesp
160 g	sweet shortcrust pastry (page 211)	6 oz
three 15 ml spoons	apricot jam	3 tablesp

Peel, core and thinly slice the cooking apples. Put them in a saucepan with the butter, the 75 g (3 oz) sugar, cinnamon, lemon rind and white wine. Cook gently until the apples are soft. Remove the cinnamon stick and mash the apples to make a puree. Allow it to cool.

Roll the pastry out to line a greased pie-tin or spring-form tin (about 20 cm/8 inches in diameter). If you are using a spring-form tin, bring the pastry well up the sides. Turn the apple puree into the lined tin. Cut the dessert apples into quarters and core them, leaving the skin on. Slice them very thinly and arrange the slices in overlapping circles on top of the puree. Scatter the remaining sugar over the apples.

Bake the pie in a moderately hot oven (190°C, 375°F, mark 5) for 30–40 minutes, until the pastry is lightly browned. If you like the apples to be slightly browned too, put the pie under a hot grill for a few seconds. Melt the apricot jam with a spoonful of water over a gentle heat. If it is very lumpy, sieve it before brushing or spooning it over the apples.

Serve the pie warm or cold.

Brandy cream biscuit

This recipe was given to me as a rum dessert but I prefer brandy. Use any liqueur.

200 g	shortcake biscuits	7 oz
60 g	unsalted butter	2½ oz
six	egg yolks	six
110 g	caster sugar	¼ lb
two 5 ml spoons	gelatine	2 teasp
150 ml	cold water	¼ pint
425 ml	double cream	14 fl oz
100 ml	brandy	3 fl oz

To make the biscuit base, crush the biscuits finely. Reserve some for decoration and add the melted butter to the rest. Stir the mixture well and press it into the base of a spring-form tin (about 20 cm/8 inches). Beat the yolks until they are light, add the sugar and continue beating.

Soak the gelatine in the cold water in a pan and then bring the mixture to the boil, stirring until the gelatine has dissolved. Pour it over the yolks and sugar, beating all the time.

Whip the cream until it is thick. Stir it into the gelatine mixture. Add the brandy and stir again. Cool the mixture until it is beginning to set before carefully spooning it onto the prepared biscuit base. Chill the pie until it is set – overnight if possible. Sprinkle the reserved biscuit crumbs in the centre before serving.

Flaming apple tarts

350 g	puff pastry (page 211)	¾ lb
450 g (approx.)	dessert apples	1 lb (approx.)
	butter	
two 15 ml spoons	caster sugar	2 tablesp
two 15 ml spoons	calvados	2 tablesp
	icing sugar	

Cut out six circles of pastry about 12 cm (4¾ inches) in diameter and place them on a moistened baking-sheet.

Peel, core and thinly slice the apples and lay the slices in an overlapping circle on each circle of pastry. Gently pull the edges of the pastry up to make a rim around the edge of each tart. Put a few small dots of butter on top of the apples and sprinkle them with caster sugar. Put the baking-sheet into a moderately hot oven (190°C, 375°F, mark 5) for about 30 minutes, until the pastry is brown and the apples are cooked.

Remove the tarts from the baking-sheet very carefully and put them onto a shallow (but not flat) flame-proof serving-dish. Warm the calvados in a soup ladle, ignite it and pour it over the tarts. Shake a sprinkling of icing sugar over the tarts before serving them. Warn your guests that they are very hot.

Orange tart

A useful basic recipe for fruit tart which can be varied according to your mood and the available fruit (see below for a version using pears).

225 g	*shortcrust pastry (page 210)*	*8 oz*
	crème pâtissière (page 213)	
three 15 ml spoons	*orange liqueur*	*3 tablesp*
three or four	*oranges*	*three or four*
one 15 ml spoon	*sugar*	*1 tablesp*
one 15 ml spoon	*water*	*1 tablesp*

Line a greased 24-cm (9½-inch) flan ring with the shortcrust pastry and bake it blind until it is crisp. Allow it to cool.

Make the crème pâtissière and leave it to cool. Stir in half the orange liqueur. Spoon the cream into the pastry shell.

Remove the peel and all the pith from the oranges and slice them very thinly. Lay the orange slices on the cream. Cut the peel into fine strips and blanch them in boiling water for five minutes. Drain the peel and return it to the pan together with the sugar and measured water. Dissolve the sugar over a medium heat and then bring the mixture to the boil. Cook it until the liquid has caramelised, stirring constantly. Stir in the remaining liqueur. Spoon the peel over the oranges.

For pear tart, use six large pears, peeled, halved, cored and poached gently in stock syrup (page 216). Substitute two 15 ml (table) spoonsful of Poire Williams or another eau-de-vie de poire for the orange liqueur. Glaze with melted, sieved apricot jam.

Puddings

A multitude of (calorific) sins are brought together here with cakes and trifles sharing the bill with old-fashioned steamed puds and even pasta – usually served at the beginning of the meal, but why not live dangerously!

Plum trifle

The handy thing about trifles is that you can put anything you like into them. This one includes plums or damsons but it is easy enough to make your own version using any fruit puree with a complementary spirit or liqueur.

225 g	trifle sponge cakes or equivalent sponge cake	½ lb
three 15 ml spoons	slivovitz or kirsch	3 tablesp
450 g	plums or damsons	1 lb
50 ml	water	2 fl oz
	sugar to taste	
	crème pâtissière (page 213)	
200 ml	whipping cream	7 fl oz
	flaked almonds, glacé cherries, angelica	

Put the sponge cake into a glass serving bowl. Pour over the slivovitz or kirsch. Make a thick puree of the plums or damsons with the water and sugar. Allow it to cool.

Spoon first the fruit puree and then the cooled crème pâtissière onto the cake. Whip the cream until it is just thick enough to spread over the crème pâtissière.

Decorate as you wish.

Pain perdu au Grand Marnier

six	thick slices of white bread	six
350 ml	milk	12 fl oz
four 5 ml spoons	sugar	4 teasp
one 5 ml spoon	vanilla essence	1 teasp
three 15 ml spoons	Grand Marnier	3 tablesp
four	eggs	four
	flour	
	butter	
	sugar	

Trim the crusts from the bread. Mix the milk with the measured sugar, the vanilla and the Grand Marnier. Pass the slices of bread through this liquid and lay them on a plate to drain. (Use a fish slice or wide spatula to lift them out of the liquid.) Beat the eggs and dip the soaked bread into them. Pass the bread through some flour, gently shaking off the excess. Fry the bread in hot butter. Sprinkle the fried bread with a little sugar before serving. Use a different liqueur if you wish.

Linguine alla mela

If you have linguine shapes, all to the good, but plain noodles will do as well.

450 g	linguine or noodles	1 lb
two	large cooking apples	two
one	lemon	one
25 g	butter	1 oz
	grated nutmeg	
150 ml	single cream	¼ pint
100 ml	brandy or marsala	3 fl oz
	salt, white pepper	

Cook the pasta *al dente* in plenty of salted water. Peel and grate the apples. Add the juice of the lemon. In a heavy pan, melt the butter and stir in the grated apples and a little grated nutmeg. As soon as the apples start to soften, stir in the cream and bring it just to the boil. Add the brandy or marsala and stir well. Remove the pan from the heat. Add a little salt and pepper. Put the drained pasta in a large serving bowl. Add the sauce, with an extra knob of butter if you wish. A few sultanas soaked in brandy make it even better.

Empire plum pudding

Christmas pudding recipes tend to be rather similar down the ages, varying in their contents only slightly from one to the other. I was taken by the concept of an Empire Plum Pudding, in *Cooking with Elizabeth Craig* (Collins 1932) where all the ingredients came from different parts of the (then) Empire. The Empire has shrunk to a Pacific island or two, but most of the ingredients are available from Commonwealth countries. For interest I give the 1932 provenance.

On a still more historic note, I was amused to read that Mrs Beeton's estimated cost of her similar Christmas pudding in 1861 was three shillings and sixpence.

This recipe makes three puddings – sufficient to feed up to twenty people, depending on their capacities.

225 g	*self-raising flour (Canada)*	*½ lb*
half 5 ml spoon	*ground cloves (Penang)*	*½ teasp*
half 5 ml spoon	*grated nutmeg (Penang)*	*½ teasp*
half 5 ml spoon	*ground mace (Penang)*	*½ teasp*
quarter 5 ml spoon	*ground cinnamon*	*¼ teasp*
half 5 ml spoon	*salt*	*½ teasp*
450 g	*shredded beef suet*	*1 lb*
350 g	*fine breadcrumbs*	*¾ lb*
450 g	*brown sugar (Barbados)*	*1 lb*
450 g	*currants (Australia)*	*1 lb*
450 g	*sultanas (Australia)*	*1 lb*
450 g	*raisins (South Africa)*	*1 lb*
two	*apples (Canada)*	*two*
225 g	*chopped candied peel (South Africa)*	*½ lb*
one	*orange (Palestine)*	*one*
one 15 ml spoon	*grapefruit juice*	*1 tablesp*
ten	*eggs*	*ten*
150 ml	*brandy (Cyprus)*	*¼ pint*
150 ml	*brown ale*	*¼ pint*
	brandy or rum butter (page 193)	

Sieve the flour, spices and salt into a large bowl (I use a preserving-pan to mix the pudding as it is large enough to give a good mix). Stir in the suet, breadcrumbs, sugar, dried fruit, peeled, cored and chopped apples, and the candied peel. Mix well before adding the juice of the orange and some grated peel, together with the grapefruit juice, the beaten eggs, the brandy and the ale. Mix everything thoroughly. Make a wish. Cover the mixture and leave it in a cool place for several hours or overnight to allow it to mellow before turning it into three greased 1.2-litre (2-pint) pudding-basins. Fill the basins only two-thirds full as the mixture rises during cooking. Cover the basins with well-buttered grease-proof paper or foil, making a pleat in the paper to allow the puddings to rise. Tie the paper or foil securely. (Use pudding-cloths if you prefer.)

Steam the puddings for seven hours (or two hours in a pressure-cooker). Make sure there is always plenty of water in the pan, topping it up with boiling water when necessary. Remove the wet paper or foil and replace it with fresh paper before storing the puddings in a dry place.

When you want to use the puddings, re-cover them with fresh buttered paper and steam them for a further three hours (or more if you like) or 50 minutes in the pressure-cooker. Serve them with brandy or rum butter.

Brandy coffee cake

175 g	*plain flour*	*6 oz*
two 5 ml spoons	*baking-powder*	*2 teasp*
one	*pinch of salt*	*one*
140 g	*brown sugar*	*5 oz*
two	*eggs*	*two*
six 15 ml spoons	*oil*	*6 tablesp*
four 15 ml spoons	*milk*	*4 tablesp*
150 ml	*strong coffee*	*1/4 pint*
110 g	*caster sugar*	*1/4 lb*
two 15 ml spoons	*brandy*	*2 tablesp*
	brandy-flavoured whipped cream	

Combine the flour, baking-powder, salt, brown sugar, eggs, oil and milk in a bowl. Add two 15 ml (table) spoonsful of the coffee and beat everything to a smooth batter.

Turn the mixture into a greased and lightly-floured cake tin (about 20 cm/8 inches) and bake the cake in a moderate oven (180°C, 350°F, mark 4) for about 40 minutes.

While the cake is baking, put the remaining coffee and the caster sugar into a pan and bring them to the boil. Simmer the liquid to reduce it to a thick syrup. Remove the pan from the heat and stir in the brandy. When the cake is baked, prick it all over with a skewer and pour the coffee syrup slowly over the hot cake. Leave the cake to cool before taking it out of the tin and serving it with brandy-flavoured whipped cream.

Negrita baba

Traditionally rum baba is made with a yeast-based cake. This version uses an ordinary cake and the less familiar dark and aromatic French (Martinique) rum.

three	eggs	three
110 g	caster sugar	1/4 lb
one	pinch of salt	one
140 g	flour	5 oz
one 5 ml spoon	baking-powder	1 teasp
three 15 ml spoons	milk	3 tablesp
100 g	butter	3½ oz
350 g	clear honey	3/4 lb
175 ml	water	6 fl oz
nine 15 ml spoons	Negrita rum	9 tablesp
	whipped cream	
	candied fruits	

Separate the eggs and beat the yolks with the sugar and salt until the mixture is thick and creamy. Sieve the flour and baking-powder onto the yolk mixture and fold it in gently. Warm the milk and butter in a pan until the butter has melted. Add this to the flour mixture and blend it in thoroughly. Beat the egg whites until they are stiff. Fold a spoonful of the beaten whites into the flour mixture. Fold in the rest of the whites.

Generously grease a small ring mould and pour the cake mixture into it. Bake it in a moderately hot oven (190°C, 375°F, mark 5) for about 15 minutes. Test the cake with a knife and remove it from the oven when it is ready.

While the cake is cooking, heat the honey, water and rum to boiling-point to make a syrup. Turn the cake out onto a shallow dish. Pour the hot syrup over it and spoon the syrup over the cake until it has all been absorbed. This can take quite a long time, so be patient.

Serve the cake cold, decorated with whipped cream and candied fruits. Flavour some more whipped cream with a little rum and serve it separately.

Use any other rum instead of the Negrita if you wish.

Crêpes

I have never come across anyone who did not like crêpes. It doesn't seem to matter how many are made, they always disappear. You can even comfort yourself that they are nutritious as well as delicious.

Spirits and liqueurs are natural partners with crêpes. A spoonful of your favourite 'digestif' is all you need to create an exciting finale to a meal. With a little more effort and imagination there is no end to the different ways you can combine crêpes with fruit, jams, crème pâtissière . . . almost anything goes.

Crêpes au liqueur

This recipe will make about twenty crêpes. They should be thin and if you are planning to fill them, cook them on only one side. Either fold them in quarters or stack them with a piece of grease-proof paper or plastic film between them.

175 g	*flour*	*6 oz*
one	*pinch of salt*	*one*
one 15 ml spoon	*sugar*	*1 tablesp*
three	*eggs*	*three*
450 ml	*milk*	*¾ pint*
two 15 ml spoons	*melted butter*	*2 tablesp*
two 15 ml spoons	*liqueur*	*2 tablesp*

Put the sieved flour, salt and sugar into a bowl and make a well in the centre. Add the eggs, one at a time, mixing them in with a fork. Slowly add the milk, beating all the time. Beat the mixture well with a whisk to remove all the lumps (or liquidise it). Stir in the melted butter and the liqueur. Leave the mixture to rest for at least an hour before making the crêpes.

To flambé the crêpes warm them through in a little butter, heat some liqueur (the same one as you used to make them) in a soup ladle and ignite it. Pour it over the crêpes in the pan and when the flames have subsided, shake a little sugar over the crêpes and serve immediately. You will need a large frying-pan and reckon to flambé about six to eight (folded) crêpes at a time, using two 15 ml (table) spoons of liqueur each time.

For crêpes normande, fill each crêpe with a spoonful of hot apple puree, and use calvados when making and flaming the crêpes.

Crêpes Pierre

Crêpes Suzette feature on many restaurant menus and if you order them you can expect to see a performance worthy of, if not Sarah Bernhardt, at least Coco the Clown. It is usually an excuse for all manner of extrovert behaviour which bears little or no resemblance to the original invention. My own version is probably even further from the truth.

twenty	crêpes (page 152) using Cointreau	twenty
15 g	butter	1/2 oz
75 g	sugar	3 oz
two	large oranges	two
one	lemon	one
two 15 ml spoons	brandy	2 tablesp
two 15 ml spoons	Cointreau	2 tablesp

Make the crêpes according to the recipe and leave them folded in quarters while you prepare the sauce. In a large frying-pan melt the butter and add the sugar, stirring until it begins to dissolve. Squeeze the oranges and lemon into the pan, using a fork. Scrape out some of the pulp of the fruit as you squeeze. When the sauce is bubbling nicely, add half the brandy and all the Cointreau. Heat it through well before adding the folded crêpes. Gently turn them in the sauce and let them warm through. Add the remaining brandy, warm it, and ignite the sauce. Bring the pan to the table and serve the crêpes as the flames subside.

This sauce should be ample for 15 to 20 crêpes. If you want to perform on a table-heater you might prefer to make the sauce in two batches as the pan will not be large enough to accommodate all the sauce at once.

Frozen sweets

Frozen sweets are popular even in the depths of winter. I always feel it is comforting to have a few of them tucked into the freezer for unexpected guests because, of course, you need only remove them from the freezer and serve them immediately. Instant pudding was never like this.

On a technical note, the use of liqueurs (or spirits) lowers the freezing-point of the mixture and therefore the dessert will melt very quickly once out of the freezer. Serve it quickly and return any that you are not using to the freezer right away.

Included here are ice-creams, frozen soufflés and other varieties of frozen sweets, all of which are specifically to be eaten direct from the freezer. Other sweets in other sections can of course be frozen and then defrosted.

Ice-cream can be changed from an everyday to a special sweet by simply pouring over a measure of liqueur. Water-ices are especially delicious with a complementary eau-de-vie, for instance, raspberry sorbet with eau-de-vie de framboise. It is worth using a 'real' ice-cream if you are going to the expense of pouring on liqueurs.

Rum ice

110 g	caster sugar	1/4 lb
50 g	candied peel	2 oz
three 15 ml spoons	rum	3 tablesp
four	eggs	four
one	pinch of cream of tartar	one
300 ml	double cream	1/2 pint

Combine the sugar, chopped peel, and rum and leave the mixture for two hours.
Separate the eggs and beat the whites with the cream of tartar until they are very stiff.

Beat the yolks until they are light and frothy and stir in the sugar mixture. Whip the cream until it is thick and fold it in gently.

Stir a spoonful of the whites lightly into the mixture to lighten it before folding in the remainder. Put the mixture into a suitable dish for freezing and freeze it, covered, for a minimum of 12 hours.

Substitute brandy or a fruit liqueur for the rum, if you wish.

Iced citrus soufflé

This is a lovely creamy sweet which in fact has no cream in it and may therefore be especially suitable for people who cannot eat cream.

six	*egg yolks*	*six*
three	*lemons*	*three*
75 g	*granulated sugar*	*3 oz*
five	*egg whites*	*five*
one	*pinch of salt*	*one*
75 g	*caster sugar*	*3 oz*
four 15 ml spoons	*orange or lemon liqueur*	*4 tablesp*
	candied fruits	

Whisk together in a heavy saucepan, the yolks, the lemon juice and a little grated rind, and the granulated sugar. Stir the mixture well with a wooden spoon over a low heat. Keep stirring until it becomes quite thick and glutinous. Take care not to let it over-heat as the yolks will scramble.

Remove the pan from the heat and plunge it into a basin of cold water. This is to cool the mixture quickly and prevent its cooking further.

Whisk the egg whites with the salt until they are very stiff. Gently fold in the caster sugar and mix together thoroughly. Scoop a spoonful of the beaten whites into the yolk mixture and fold it in very lightly. Continue to do this with the rest of the beaten whites until both mixtures are incorporated. Add the liqueur and mix it through carefully. Turn the mixture into individual pots or one large dish. Cover with foil and freeze for at least six hours.

Before serving, decorate with pieces of candied fruit.

Frozen orange dessert

three	*egg yolks*	*three*
250 g	*caster sugar*	*9 oz*
three 15 ml spoons	*water*	*3 tablesp*
450 ml	*whipping cream*	*¾ pint*
five 15 ml spoons	*orange liqueur*	*5 tablesp*
	candied fruits or	
	crystallised violets	

Beat the yolks until they are light and creamy. Put the sugar and water into a saucepan and cook over a low heat until the mixture becomes a syrup. Stir constantly and continue cooking until a thread is formed when the syrup is dropped from a fork. Remove the pan from the heat and very slowly add the syrup to the beaten yolks, beating all the time. Continue to beat for a further five minutes (two minutes by machine). Sometimes the mixture becomes rather hard and crystalline, but this smooths out when it is mixed with the cream and subsequently frozen.

Whip the cream until it is thick and fold it into the egg and sugar mixture. Add the liqueur. Turn the mixture into individual dishes or one large dish. Cover with foil and freeze for a minimum of 12 hours. Serve decorated with candied fruit or crystallised violets and more whipped cream if you wish.

Strawberry ice-cream

225 g	*strawberries*	*½ lb*
110 g	*icing sugar*	*¼ lb*
three 15 ml spoons	*orange liqueur*	*3 tablesp*
300 ml	*whipping cream*	*½ pint*

Liquidise the strawberries. Add the sugar and liqueur and stir until the sugar has dissolved. Whip the cream until it is thick. Fold it into the fruit mixture. Put it into a suitable dish for freezing and freeze it, covered, for a minimum of six hours. Remove from the freezer ten minutes before it is required.

You can sieve the fruit before adding the other ingredients but I don't find it necessary, and inevitably you lose some flavour by doing this. Dry-frozen berries are successful in this recipe. If the colour is rather faded, add a drop of cochineal.

Marsala ice-cream

This recipe requires candied fruits *not* candied peel. They make delicious holiday souvenirs or Christmas presents.

four 15 ml spoons	chopped candied fruits	4 tablesp
125 ml	marsala	4 fl oz
four	egg yolks	four
three 15 ml spoons	caster sugar	3 tablesp
300 ml	whipping cream	½ pint

Soak the chopped candied fruits in the marsala for two hours.

Put the egg yolks and sugar into a heavy-bottomed pan. Strain the marsala from the candied fruits into the pan (reserving the fruits) and mix thoroughly with a whisk. Place the pan over a low heat and continue to whisk until the mixture becomes foamy. Take care not to overheat the pan as the yolks will scramble. Put the pan into a basin of cold water to cool it down quickly and stop the cooking process. Stir the mixture until it is cool.

Whip the cream and fold it into the cooled mixture. Add the reserved candied fruits and stir them through the cream. Put the mixture into a suitable dish for freezing.

Freeze, covered, for a minimum of 12 hours.

Madeira and raisin sorbet

110 g	raisins	¼ lb
100 ml	madeira	3 fl oz
600 ml	water	1 pint
175 g	sugar	6 oz
four 15 ml spoons	lemon juice	4 tablesp
one	egg white	one

Soak the raisins in the madeira for two hours. Make a stock syrup with the water and sugar (page 216) and leave it to cool.

Mix the cooled syrup with the raisins and madeira. Add the lemon juice and stir thoroughly. Put the mixture into a container suitable for the freezer and freeze it for at least six hours. Liquidise or process the frozen mixture (in two batches if necessary). Add the stiffly-beaten egg white to the mixture and blend it in. Return the sorbet to the freezer and leave it for at least 12 hours.

Serve the sorbet direct from the freezer since it melts very quickly.

Frozen Christmas pudding

Not everyone likes the traditional Christmas pudding, especially after turkey with all the trimmings. For them, or just as a change, or if you are celebrating Christmas in the Antipodes, try this easy alternative. You should use either a home-made ice-cream for this or a really good commercial one. It is not worth wasting the ingredients on a mediocre ice-cream.

175 g	*mixed cake fruit or the equivalent of raisins, sultanas, currants and mixed peel*	*6 oz*
three	*small pieces of candied fruit*	*three*
four 15 ml spoons	*brandy*	*4 tablesp*
40 g	*flaked almonds*	*1½ oz*
1 litre	*vanilla ice-cream*	*1¾ pints*

Mix the cake fruit with the finely-chopped candied fruit. Pour on the brandy and leave the mixture to macerate for three or four hours.

Add the flaked almonds and stir the fruit and brandy mixture into the slightly-softened ice-cream. Mix everything together very well. Put the mixture into a pudding basin, cover it, and freeze it overnight.

Serve it direct from the freezer as it defrosts rather quickly because of the brandy in it. Turn it out onto a deep plate.

Austrian punch sauce (page 192) goes well with this 'pudding'.

Creams, jellies, syllabubs and mousses

There are subtle distinctions in culinary terms between a charlotte and a Bavarian cream, a cold soufflé and a mousse, a fool and a syllabub, but for my purposes they are all quite safely gathered together in this collection.

What I find so appealing about a syllabub is not only the speed with which you can conjure it up, but also the almost endless possible variations on the theme. I give my own favourites, but recommend you try your hand at inventing your own, with whatever alcoholic liquid you have to hand. Certainly any liqueur would be suitable, and there is no limit to the variety of wines that might be used. Even red wine, which I had thought of excepting from this rule, is required for the Medieval syllabub.

Commercial jellies can be useful as a base on which to build more interesting sweets, but it is possible to make a good variety of tasty jellies by using well-flavoured wines or liqueurs plus gelatine. A mousse is just a step away, with the addition of eggs and cream.

Blackcurrant cream

450 g	blackcurrants (fresh or frozen)	1 lb
300 ml	water	1/2 pint
110 g	sugar	1/4 lb
four 5 ml spoons	gelatine	4 teasp
three 15 ml spoons	eau-de-vie de poire	3 tablesp
225 g	trifle sponge cakes	1/2 lb
150 ml	double cream	1/4 pint

Cook the washed blackcurrants with the water and sugar. You needn't strip them off the stalk. When they are soft, rub them through a sieve. Return the puree to the pan and sprinkle the gelatine over it. Stir the mixture over a gentle heat until the gelatine is dissolved. Pour the puree into a bowl and leave it to cool. Add the eau-de-vie and refrigerate until the puree is just beginning to set.

Meanwhile line a small spring-form cake tin (about 20 cm/8 inches) with the sponge cakes. As they are rather thick, slice them in half horizontally. Use the soft pieces to cover the bottom of the tin.

When the mixture is partially set, pour half into the tin. Leave it to set in the refrigerator. Whip the cream and add it to the remaining mixture. Mix together until smooth. Spoon the creamy mixture into the tin when the first layer is set and refrigerate for at least four hours, overnight if possible.

Carefully trim off any cake which comes above the level of the cream. Remove the ring, leaving the bottom of the tin in place. Serve the sweet in wedges, decorated with fruit or jam, if you wish. The two tones look very pretty.

This is particularly delicious with eau-de-vie de poire but if you don't happen to have any, try Crème de Cassis or calvados.

Apricot brandy cream (6–8)

450 g	*dried apricots*	*1 lb*
four	*eggs*	*four*
50 g	*caster sugar*	*2 oz*
300 ml	*double cream*	*½ pint*
two 15 ml spoons	*brandy*	*2 tablesp*

Soak the apricots overnight in enough water to cover them. On the following day, cook them in the water in which they have soaked until they are tender. Either rub them through a sieve or liquidise them to make a puree. Separate the eggs. Beat the yolks with the sugar until they are light and fluffy. Whisk the whites until they are stiff. Whip the cream until it is thick.

Fold the apricot puree, the brandy and the cream into the beaten yolks. Mix well. Take a spoonful of the whites and gently stir it into the mixture to lighten it. Fold in the rest of the whites. Spoon the mixture into small pots or glasses. Chill the cream and decorate it with flaked almonds if you wish.

This cream freezes very well. Defrost it before serving.

Strawberry Bavarian cream

two 15 ml spoons	gelatine	2 tablesp
50 ml	cold water	2 fl oz
six	egg yolks	six
110 g	caster sugar	¼ lb
300 ml	milk	½ pint
one 5 ml spoon	vanilla essence	1 teasp
450 g	strawberries	1 lb
three 15 ml spoons	kirsch	3 tablesp
225 ml	double cream	8 fl oz

Soak the gelatine in the cold water. Beat the egg yolks with the sugar until the mixture is light and fluffy. Scald the milk and pour it onto the egg mixture, beating it all the time. Transfer the mixture to a pan and cook it over a gentle heat until it begins to thicken. Add the soaked gelatine and the vanilla, stirring until the gelatine has dissolved. Sieve the custard into a bowl and leave it to cool and thicken, but not to set. Liquidise or sieve the strawberries. When the custard has cooled, add the pureed fruit and the kirsch. Whip the cream until it is thick and fold it into the custard and fruit mixture. Pour the mixture into a moistened mould. Refrigerate it, covered, for at least four hours before turning it out.

This cream freezes very well. Defrost it overnight in the refrigerator before serving. Strawberries don't freeze well whole but pureed they are excellent. I keep a stock of unsweetened puree in the freezer and it is ideal for this recipe.

Dundee syllabub

300 ml	double cream	½ pint
two 15 ml spoons	whisky	2 tablesp
two 15 ml spoons	caster sugar	2 tablesp
two 15 ml spoons	orange marmalade	2 tablesp

Whisk the cream, whisky and sugar together until thick. Chop the marmalade if it is very chunky and stir it through the cream. Spoon the mixture into small pots or glasses. Refrigerate until chilled.

Coffee chocolate syllabub

300 ml	*double cream*	*½ pint*
three 15 ml spoons	*Royal French Coffee-Chocolate Liqueur*	*3 tablesp*
50 g	*caster sugar*	*2 oz*
two 15 ml spoons	*strong black coffee*	*2 tablesp*
	grated chocolate	

Combine all the ingredients except the chocolate in a large bowl. Whisk until the mixture is thick and smooth. Spoon it into individual glasses and decorate it with a little grated chocolate. Refrigerate until chilled. Substitute another coffee liqueur if you wish.

Sherry syllabub

one	*orange*	*one*
one	*lemon*	*one*
50 g	*caster sugar*	*2 oz*
50 ml	*sweet sherry*	*2 fl oz*
300 ml	*whipping cream*	*½ pint*

Grate the rinds and squeeze the juice of the orange and lemon into a bowl. Add the sugar, sherry and cream. Whisk everything together until it is thick and smooth. Spoon into individual pots or glasses. Refrigerate until chilled.

Medieval syllabub

300 ml	*double cream*	*½ pint*
150 ml	*red wine*	*¼ pint*
100 ml	*light ale*	*3 fl oz*
50 g	*caster sugar*	*2 oz*
	grated nutmeg	

Combine the cream, wine, ale and sugar and whisk them together until the mixture is thick. Spoon the syllabub into glasses and refrigerate until chilled. Sprinkle a little nutmeg on top just before serving.

Wine and brandy syllabub

one	*lemon*	*one*
100 ml	*sweet white wine*	*3 fl oz*
two 15 ml spoons	*brandy*	*2 tablesp*
50 g	*caster sugar*	*2 oz*
300 ml	*double cream*	*½ pint*
	grated nutmeg	

The day before the syllabub is required, put the thinly-pared rind of the lemon in a bowl, together with the juice, the wine and the brandy. Leave overnight.

The next day, strain the liquid into a bowl. Add the sugar and cream and whisk until the mixture is thick and smooth. Spoon it into individual pots or glasses, and sprinkle a little grated nutmeg over each one. Refrigerate until chilled.

Raspberry fool

Raspberries freeze very well and it is always pleasant to serve a raspberry sweet in the middle of winter. If you use dry-frozen berries for this, drain off the juice before adding them to the cream. (Commercially-frozen berries in syrup are not suitable unless you adjust the amount of sugar.)

50 g	*caster sugar*	*2 oz*
350 g	*raspberries*	*¾ lb*
four 15 ml spoons	*kirsch*	*4 tablesp*
450 ml	*whipping cream*	*¾ pint*

Sprinkle the sugar over the raspberries. Add the kirsch to the cream and whip it until it is thick. Reserve a few raspberries for decoration and fold the remainder gently into the cream. Spoon the fool into individual glasses or one large serving dish. Decorate with the reserved raspberries. Use eau-de-vie de framboise instead of kirsch if you wish.

Charlotte à l'Avicenna

This intriguingly-named sweet was the first-prize-winner in a national competition sponsored by a liqueur house for an original recipe using the products of the house. The winner named his dish after an Arab philosopher, Avicenna, who wrote in the 10th century about the distillation of two alcoholic products. This charlotte requires two different liqueurs, naturally complementary in flavour.

one	orange	one
two 15 ml spoons	Royal Orange-Chocolate Liqueur	2 tablesp
15 g	stem ginger	½ oz
one 15 ml spoon	ginger syrup	1 tablesp
two 15 ml spoons	Royal Ginger-Chocolate Liqueur	2 tablesp
half	packet (135 g/4¾ oz) orange jelly	half
	angelica, glacé cherries	
one 15 ml spoon	gelatine	1 tablesp
two 15 ml spoons	water	2 tablesp
two	eggs	two
two and a half 15 ml spoons	caster sugar	2½ tablesp
175 ml	milk	6 fl oz
	red and yellow food colouring	
225 ml	whipping cream	8 fl oz
	brandy-snaps (page 212)	

Grate the zest from the orange. Peel the orange, remove the pith and divide the flesh into segments. Put the zest, the orange segments and the orange liqueur into a bowl and leave them to marinate while you continue with the recipe.

Dice the ginger finely and marinate it together with the syrup and the ginger liqueur. (If you prefer, you can use 25 g/1 oz of ginger marmalade instead of the ginger and syrup.)

Make up the orange jelly according to the instructions on the packet. Pour a little jelly onto the bottom of the charlotte mould and when it is beginning to set, carefully arrange the orange segments in it, with some strips of angelica and cherry to make a pattern. Carefully spoon on some more jelly and leave the mould in the refrigerator until it has set.

Soak the gelatine in the cold water. Mix the egg yolks and sugar together well. Scald the milk and pour it onto the egg-yolk mixture, beating all the time. Return the mixture to the saucepan over a gentle heat and stir it until it thickens, taking care not to let it boil. Add the soaked gelatine and stir until it has dissolved. Strain the custard and divide it into two bowls.

Flavour one half of the mixture with the diced ginger mixture and the other half with the orange liqueur mixture and any remaining orange segments, finely diced. Colour the orange mixture with red and yellow food colouring to a pale orange tone.

Whisk the egg whites and whip the cream until it is thick. As the two custards begin to set, gently fold half of the egg whites and half of the cream into each of them. Pour the orange mixture into the prepared mould and place it in the refrigerator to set. (Leave the ginger one at room temperature.)

Carefully spoon the ginger mixture onto the set orange one. Return the mould to the refrigerator, overnight if possible but for at least three hours.

Unmould the charlotte onto a flat dish and, if you wish, serve it with brandy-snaps.

Charlotte au liqueur

This is a very useful all-purpose dessert which can be made with any liqueur you have available.

four 15 ml spoons	chopped candied fruit	4 tablesp
four 15 ml spoons	liqueur	4 tablesp
five	egg yolks	five
110 g	caster sugar	1/4 lb
450 ml	milk	3/4 pint
one and a half 15 ml spoons	gelatine	1 1/2 tablesp
three 15 ml spoons	water	3 tablesp
450 ml	whipping cream	3/4 pint
75 g	boudoir biscuits	3 oz

Put the candied fruit into a bowl and pour over the liqueur. Leave it to soak for about two hours. In a bowl, beat the egg yolks with the sugar until they are light and frothy. Pour the heated milk onto the egg mixture, stirring constantly. Place the bowl over a pan of boiling water and stir until the custard thickens a little. Soak the gelatine in the water for a few minutes. Add it to the custard and stir until the gelatine has dissolved. Strain this mixture into a clean bowl and leave it to cool.

When the custard has cooled, whip the cream until it is thick. Fold it into the cooled mixture. Add the candied fruit and the liqueur in which it has soaked. Leave this mixture in the refrigerator, covered, until it is beginning to set. Cut a circle of grease-proof paper or foil to fit the bottom of a small charlotte mould. Line the sides of the mould with the biscuits. (A dab of butter on the edges of each one helps them to stick.) When the mixture is beginning to set, spoon it into the prepared mould. Refrigerate it until it is firm, preferably overnight. Carefully unmould the charlotte and remove the paper from the top.

I have used green Chartreuse, Bénédictine, Mandarine and other orange-flavoured liqueurs, all to good effect. You can enhance the appearance by adding a little food colouring if you like.

Lemon wine cream

This sweet can be used as a filling for cakes or flans.

125 ml	dry white wine	4 fl oz
50 ml	water	2 fl oz
75 g	sugar	3 oz
two	lemons	two
25 g	cornflour	1 oz
two	egg yolks	two
150 ml	whipping cream	1/4 pint

Put the wine, water, sugar and the juice of the lemons into a heavy saucepan. Add a little grated lemon rind, the cornflour, and the egg yolks. Mix everything thoroughly and place the pan over medium heat. Bring the mixture to the boil, stirring from time to time. When it is thick, remove the pan from the heat and transfer the mixture to a bowl. Leave it to cool.

Whip the cream until it is thick and fold it into the cooled mixture. Spoon the sweet into a serving-bowl or individual dishes and chill until required.

Velvet wine cream

five	*egg yolks*	*five*
200 ml	*sweet white wine*	*7 fl oz*
four 15 ml spoons	*caster sugar*	*4 tablesp*
four	*egg whites*	*four*
300 ml	*whipping cream*	*1/2 pint*

Mix the yolks, the wine and the sugar together well in a small saucepan. Cook them gently over a low heat, stirring constantly until the mixture is thick. Remove the pan from the heat and plunge it into a basin of cold water to cool it quickly.

Whisk the egg whites until they are stiff and whip the cream until it is thick. Fold the cream into the yolk mixture, mixing it in thoroughly. Take a spoonful of the whites and fold them into the yolk mixture to lighten it. Gently fold in the rest of the whites.

Spoon the mixture into glasses and refrigerate it, covered, until required.

Decorate the cream with finely-chopped nuts if you wish.

Chocolate cream

You can use different liqueurs in this – any strongly-flavoured orange liqueur would do (for example, Van der Hum), or try mint-chocolate or kirsch.

350 g	*plain chocolate*	*3/4 lb*
three	*eggs*	*three*
three 15 ml spoons	*caster sugar*	*3 tablesp*
50 ml	*Mandarine Napoléon*	*2 fl oz*
150 ml	*double cream*	*1/4 pint*

Melt the chocolate in a bowl over boiling water. Separate the eggs. Beat the yolks and slowly add the melted chocolate, beating constantly. Add the sugar and stir until it has dissolved. Reserve one spoonful of the liqueur and add the rest to the chocolate mixture. Leave this to cool.

Whisk the whites until they are stiff. Stir a spoonful of the whites into the chocolate mixture to lighten it and then add the rest of the whites, folding them in carefully. Turn the mixture into a small pudding basin, lined with lightly-oiled foil. Leave the mixture to set, preferably overnight, in the refrigerator.

Just before serving, add the reserved liqueur to the cream and whip until it is stiff. Invert the set chocolate onto a plate and carefully peel off the foil. Cover the chocolate with the cream. Serve very cold.

Royal Ginger-Chocolate mousse

Orange liqueur could be used instead of the ginger-chocolate.

four	*eggs*	*four*
four 15 ml spoons	*caster sugar*	*4 tablesp*
four 5 ml spoons	*gelatine*	*4 teasp*
three 15 ml spoons	*boiling water*	*3 tablesp*
four 15 ml spoons	*whipping cream*	*¹/₄ pint*
two	*pieces of stem ginger*	*two*
150 ml	*Royal Ginger-Chocolate Liqueur*	*4 tablesp*

Separate the eggs. Beat the yolks with the sugar until they are very light and creamy. Dissolve the gelatine in the boiling water. Whisk the whites until they are stiff. Add the cream to the yolks and sugar, along with the chopped ginger and the liqueur. Quickly add the gelatine mixture, straining it, if necessary, to remove any lumps.

Stir a spoonful of the whites into the yolk mixture to lighten it and then add the rest of the whites, folding them in carefully. Spoon the mousse into individual pots or a serving bowl. Refrigerate it, covered, until required. Decorate with more chopped ginger or grated chocolate if you like.

This mousse freezes very well. Allow at least two hours at room temperature to defrost.

You can turn the mousse into a sort of cake by lining a spring-form tin (about 20 cm/ 8 inches) with boudoir biscuits and spooning the mixture into the tin. Leave it to set.

Wine jelly

Use Asti Spumante and Muscatel grapes for a lovely fruity flavour.

one 15 ml spoon	*gelatine*	*1 tablesp*
three 15 ml spoons	*cold water*	*3 tablesp*
500 ml	*sweet white wine*	*18 fl oz*
two 15 ml spoons	*caster sugar*	*2 tablesp*
	grapes	

Soak the gelatine in the water. Pour half the wine into a pan and add the sugar. Add the softened gelatine and heat it gently, stirring until it has dissolved. Bring the mixture to the boil, remove it from the heat, and add the rest of the wine. Pour the jelly into a moistened mould and when it is cool, refrigerate it until it is beginning to set. Stir in some halved grapes and leave the jelly to set. Unmould; serve with cream if you wish.

For orange wine jelly, increase the gelatine to one and a half 15 ml (table) spoons, and use 150 ml (¼ pint) each of orange juice and sweet white wine, and 300 ml (½ pint) of water. You may need to increase the sugar slightly if the juice is rather sour.

Rum chocolate pots

This is a very rich sweet and a little goes a long way. Substitute orange or coffee liqueur, or brandy, if you prefer.

25 g	*unsalted butter*	*1 oz*
225 g	*plain chocolate*	*½ lb*
125 ml	*milk*	*4 fl oz*
50 ml	*rum*	*2 fl oz*
two	*eggs*	*two*

Melt the butter and chocolate in a bowl over boiling water. Leave the mixture to cool a little. Scald the milk and add the rum to it. Separate the eggs, adding the milk to the yolks, very slowly, stirring constantly. Beat the whites until they are stiff.

Pour the milk mixture onto the chocolate and stir well. Stir in a spoonful of the whites to lighten the mixture and then gently fold in the rest. Spoon the mixture into pots and refrigerate them. Decorate with whipped cream and grated chocolate if you wish.

Zabaglione

This always strikes me as a magical sweet, a marvellous fluffy confection whisked up from such apparently ordinary ingredients. It is of course traditionally made with marsala wine, but a fair imitation can be made using sherry and, on the same principle, you can make a lovely sauce, substituting a sparkling wine for the marsala.

The problem of how to serve zabaglione cold at first seemed to me insuperable since it has a nasty habit of deflating within minutes of being spooned into its serving dish. It may be cheating to add a little gelatine, but it certainly stabilises the mixture, and for a harassed host or hostess it saves the last-minute panic of whisking up the sweet and getting it to the table before it collapses. Perhaps best of all of this type is the zabaglione-like marsala ice-cream (page 157).

Hot zabaglione

An electric mixer is a great help but a good whisk is even better.

six	*egg yolks*	*six*
two 15 ml spoons	*caster sugar*	*2 tablesp*
six 15 ml spoons	*marsala*	*6 tablesp*

Combine the ingredients in a large bowl and whisk them well. Place the bowl over a pan of simmering water and keep whisking until the mixture has become very foamy. It will have increased in bulk and swollen into soft mounds. Remove it from the heat as soon as it gets to this stage. Do not let it go dark and sticky, which will happen if it is allowed to cook too long. Quickly spoon it into glasses and serve it immediately. It will sink and separate if left for more than a minute or two.

Serve with boudoir biscuits or langues de chat.

Cold zabaglione

two 5 ml spoons	gelatine	2 teasp
three 15 ml spoons	water	3 tablesp
six	egg yolks	six
four 15 ml spoons	caster sugar	4 tablesp
150 ml	marsala	1/4 pint

Leave the gelatine to soak in the cold water for a few minutes. Put the bowl over a pan of simmering water and stir until the gelatine has dissolved. Remove the bowl from the heat. Mix the remaining ingredients together in a second bowl and place it in turn over the pan of simmering water. Whisk until the mixture is light and frothy (as for hot zabaglione). Stir in the dissolved gelatine and remove the bowl from the heat.

Beat the mixture until it is cool and spoon it into individual glasses. Refrigerate until required.

Serve with brandy-snaps (page 212) or other crisp biscuits.

Zabaglione mousse

six	eggs	six
four 15 ml spoons	caster sugar	4 tablesp
six 15 ml spoons	marsala	6 tablesp
450 g	strawberries or raspberries	1 lb

Separate the eggs and beat the yolks with the sugar until very thick. Add the marsala and mix it in well. Put the mixture into a heavy-bottomed pan over a very low heat, stirring it constantly until it becomes thick and creamy. Cool this cream and refrigerate it for several hours.

Just before serving, whisk the egg whites until they are very stiff and fold them into the prepared cream. Gently fold in the fruit (slice the strawberries if they are large) and serve the mousse immediately.

Fruit

The addition of liqueurs or spirits to a fruit salad lifts something quite ordinary into the realms of the very special. Fruit-based liqueurs are the obvious choice, but spirits and eaux-de-vie are also excellent. A somewhat elaborate, but potent, fruit cocktail can be achieved by marinating various fruits in their complementary liqueur or spirit and then combining them all together: thus, apples marinated with calvados, cherries in Maraschino, pears in Poire Williams, plums in quetsch or slivovitz, apricots in brandy, and so on. I'm not sure whether one should eat or drink this concoction.

The simple combination of fruits with liqueurs can be taken a step further and with a little more effort some delicious sweets can be created. Pineapple, usually married to kirsch, tastes even better with a whisky-based liqueur (Drambuie or Glayva, say) and bananas respond as happily to sweet sherry as to rum.

Flambéed fruit

Flambéeing is an art. I was reminded of this fact when I witnessed a head waiter in a French hotel showing off his talents with the crêpes and liqueurs. Unfortunately he overdid the drama a little and managed to ignite not only the spirit but also his eyelashes and a rather fetching coiffure. The moral of the tale is that when playing with fire, do so judiciously and leave the theatrical embellishments to circus artistes. This is not to say that it need be a dangerous pastime, and certainly the flambéeing of fruits can not only add excitement to a meal but also transform a mundane piece of fruit into an interesting sweet. If you have no table spirit stove, you can cook perfectly well on the kitchen stove and transport the finished product to the table.

The same method of flambéeing applies whichever fruit you choose. The most successful fruits I have tried are peaches, pineapple, bananas and oranges. Prepare the fruit before you begin, removing the skin and slicing it.

The amount of fruit you can flambé depends of course on the size of your pan. Most table-heaters do not accommodate a very large pan and you should take care not to crowd it if you are going to ignite the spirit in the pan. You should be able to make two or three portions in an average-sized frying-pan.

Melt a knob of butter in the pan. Add a 15 ml (table) spoonful of sugar and stir it round until it melts. Place the fruit in the pan and turn it gently to coat it and warm it through. Pour over one to two 15 ml (table) spoonsful of spirit or liqueur. When it is warm, ignite the sauce. Shake the pan gently and let the flames subside before you serve the fruit with the sauce – and with ice-cream or cake or pancakes too, if you wish.

The liqueur or spirit you choose depends on the fruit. Brandy goes with anything, but particularly well with peaches and apricots. Maraschino is also good with these. Bananas almost invariably go with rum, pineapple with kirsch, oranges with any orange-flavoured liqueur, apples with calvados, and so on.

Macerated strawberries

You may agree with me that there is very little one can do to a strawberry that can possibly improve on its raw state. However, occasionally a glut in a good year means a surfeit of strawberries in the kitchen, and then you might try this most divine way of dressing up the simple berry, rather less fattening than strawberries Romanoff.

700 g	*firm strawberries*	*1½ lb*
two 15 ml spoons	*vodka*	*2 tablesp*
two 15 ml spoons	*rum*	*2 tablesp*
two 15 ml spoons	*curaçao*	*2 tablesp*
	icing sugar to taste	
	whipped cream	

Place the strawberries in a glass bowl. Pour on the vodka, rum and curaçao. Sprinkle on a little icing sugar and carefully mix it in. Add more sugar if necessary. Leave the bowl in the refrigerator for several hours. Serve with whipped cream.

Stuffed peaches

25 g	blanched almonds	1 oz
25 g	blanched hazelnuts	1 oz
50 g	sugar	2 oz
six	peaches	six
110 g	vanilla sugar (page 218)	1/4 lb
125 ml	sweet white wine	4 fl oz
300 ml	double cream	1/2 pint
three 15 ml spoons	apricot brandy	3 tablesp

To make the praline, put the almonds and hazelnuts into a pan with the sugar. Place the pan over a gentle heat and let the sugar melt, stirring constantly, until it turns a light golden colour. Oil a flat baking-sheet or marble slab and turn the melted sugar mixture onto it. Leave it to set really hard. Crush the praline in a liquidiser or with a rolling-pin. (It need not be very finely crushed for this recipe.)

Peel and halve the peaches, removing the stones. Poach them in a syrup made from the sugar and wine. Drain and chill the peaches. Reduce the syrup until it is very thick.

Whip the cream and fold in the crushed praline and two-thirds of the liqueur. Stuff the chilled peaches with the cream-nut mixture. Add the remaining apricot brandy to the syrup and pour it over the peaches. Chill them for a further hour or more before serving.

Failing vanilla sugar, add half a 5 ml (tea) spoonful of vanilla essence to the syrup.

Peaches in sparkling wine

six	peaches	six
75 g	caster sugar	3 oz
one	lemon	one
one	orange	one
300 ml	sparkling wine	1/2 pint

Peel and slice the peaches. Place them in a bowl and sprinkle them with the sugar. Squeeze the lemon and orange and add the juice to the peaches, together with a little grated rind. Pour over the sparkling wine and chill for at least four hours.

You could use drained, tinned peaches, omitting the sugar, and still white wine instead of sparkling – but the dish might lose its sparkle too.

Ciliegie al barolo

The cherry season always seems to be over before I've realised it has begun. This recipe should be made with morellos if possible. I have found that good dry-frozen cherries (uncooked) can be used very effectively.

175 g	sugar	6 oz
one	strip of orange peel	one
one	pinch of ground cinnamon	one
one 15 ml spoon	redcurrant jelly	1 tablesp
150 ml	full-bodied red wine	¼ pint
700 g	cherries, morellos or red	1½ lb

Put everything except the cherries into a pan and heat the mixture gently to dissolve the sugar. Bring the liquid to the boil and cook it for one minute. Add the washed cherries to the pan. Simmer them for ten minutes. Strain the liquid into a second pan and boil it rapidly to reduce it by half, before pouring it over the cherries in a serving-dish.

Serve either hot or cold, with sponge cake, ice-cream or whipped cream.

If you are using frozen cherries, they may be already pitted, and you will thus need only 450 g (1 lb).

Candied clementines

six	clementines	six
300 ml	water	½ pint
225 g	sugar	½ lb
one	small cinnamon stick	one
two 15 ml spoons	Mandarine Napoléon	2 tablesp

Place the clementines in a pan and cover them with water. Bring them to the boil and cook them for ten minutes, boiling all the time. Drain the fruit and leave it to cool a little. Prick the clementines with a fork.

Heat the measured water with the sugar and cinnamon to dissolve the sugar. Put the clementines in, with a plate on top of them to hold them under the liquid. Bring the syrup to the boil, cover the pan, reduce the heat and simmer for about half an hour.

Leave the fruit to cool before stirring in the liqueur. Serve with cream if you wish.

These clementines will keep for well over a week in a sealed dish in the refrigerator. You should be able to eat the whole fruit, peel and all, but it depends on the clementines: some peel is too tough to eat, however long you cook it. Use very small clementines for this as they are more compact and softer-skinned than the larger varieties. Other liqueurs flavoured with orange peel can be used, for example, the Cypriot Filfar.

Pears in honey and brandy

four 15 ml spoons	clear honey	4 tablesp
175 ml	water	6 fl oz
1 kg	pears	2 lb
three 15 ml spoons	brandy	3 tablesp

Place the honey and water in a shallow saucepan and heat it gently to dissolve the honey. Peel and core the pears, leaving them whole if they are small. Add them to the pan, cover, and cook them gently until they are tender. (The time depends upon the ripeness of the fruit.)

Remove the pears from the syrup and put them into a glass bowl. Add the brandy to the syrup and pour it over the pears. Serve either hot or cold, with cream if you wish.

Mulled fruit salad

Any fruit you have to hand can be added to this. In winter I put in frozen fruits. The selection given here is just a guide – use your imagination.

300 ml	dry cider	½ pint
150 ml	orange juice	¼ pint
six 15 ml spoons	clear honey	6 tablesp
one	piece of cinnamon stick	one
one	piece of root ginger	one
110 g	plums	¼ lb
two	apples	two
two	oranges	two
two	pears	two
two	apricots	two
two	peaches	two
two	bananas	two
225 g	cherries	½ lb

Put the cider, orange juice, honey and spices into a pan and simmer them gently for ten minutes. Peel, core and slice the fruits as appropriate, and add them to the syrup. Warm them through over gentle heat for five minutes. Serve with cream if you wish.

Baked apples

six	medium-sized cooking apples	six
twelve	sugar lumps	twelve
225 ml	red vermouth	8 fl oz
125 ml	water	4 fl oz

Core the apples, and with a pointed knife score a line round the middle of each, just to cut the skin. Dip each sugar lump into the vermouth and place two lumps inside each apple. Put the apples in a shallow oven-proof dish. Pour the remaining vermouth and the water round the apples, and cook them, uncovered, in a moderate oven (180°C, 350°F, mark 4) for about half an hour, until they are tender. (Some varieties will require longer.) As an alternative, stuff the cored apples with 175 g (6 oz) sultanas or raisins soaked briefly in sweet white wine and combined with 50 g (2 oz) butter, 75 g (3 oz) sugar and a little grated lemon rind. Pour over 125 ml (4 fl oz) sweet white wine and cook as above.

Sauces

As everyone knows, the sauce chefs in great restaurants are very important members of the team, and rightly so, for a sauce can make or mar a meal.

To make a fine sauce requires a great deal of effort, patience and the best ingredients, all of which might or might not be readily to hand in your house. It is worth acquiring a repertoire of all-purpose sauces, plus a few more specialised ones, as they can transform an ordinary dish into something exotic.

Many of the recipes in this book require a marinade for the meat. I include one all-purpose marinade in this section as well as one for barbecues.

Sweet sauces are represented here too but the bulk are savoury ones, since they are so useful for dressing up simply-cooked food. Most sauces (except the delicate butter sauces) freeze well, and it is always worth making extra quantities to save for another day.

In a diet-conscious family it may be helpful to be able to cook grills or steaks for the slimmers, and provide a sauce for those who are not counting calories.

Brown sauce or sauce espagnole

This quantity yields about 300 ml (½ pint) of sauce.

25 g	*butter*	*1 oz*
25 g	*flour*	*1 oz*
600 ml	*beef stock (page 214)*	*1 pint*
one	*slice of unsmoked bacon*	*one*
one	*medium-sized onion*	*one*
one	*carrot*	*one*
one	*stick of celery*	*one*
one–two	*mushrooms*	*one–two*
one 15 ml spoon	*tomato puree*	*1 tablesp*
	a few peppercorns	
one	*bouquet garni (page 216)*	*one*
	salt, pepper	

Make a brown roux (page 217) with the butter and flour and blend into it three-quarters of the stock. Bring this to the boil, stirring it continuously, and let it simmer gently. Chop the bacon and vegetables and fry them until they are brown. Add them to the sauce with the tomato puree, the peppercorns and the bouquet garni, and continue to simmer it, partially covered, for at least two hours so that it reduces. From time to time skim off the fat which rises by adding a little of the remaining cold stock, bringing the sauce back to the boil and skimming the surface. When the sauce is reduced by at least half, rub it through a sieve into a clean pan and add some seasoning.

Quick brown sauce

This is frankly a cheat. Faced with the problem of making the basis for various sauces, I balked at the idea of spending days over the stove. Even a couple of hours is a luxury we cannot always afford, so an alternative to the excellent brown sauce opposite (reprinted from earlier *Good Food Guide* cookery books) seems useful. If you have no home-made stock, use a good stock cube, but check the seasoning before using the sauce. This recipe makes about 300 ml (½ pint) of basic sauce.

25 g	butter	1 oz
one	small onion	one
one	small carrot	one
one	stick of celery	one
two 15 ml spoons	flour	2 tablesp
600 ml	beef stock (page 214)	1 pint
one 5 ml spoon	tomato puree	1 teasp
	salt, pepper	

Melt the butter and add the finely-chopped vegetables. Cook them for five minutes, stirring from time to time, until they are light brown. Add the flour and mix it in well, stirring it for about five minutes until it is nut-brown.

Add the stock, stirring constantly, and then the tomato puree, stirring until it is dissolved. Bring the sauce to the boil and cook it, uncovered, at a gentle boil for 15 minutes.

Strain the sauce through a fine sieve, pressing the vegetables well to extract all the liquid. Check the seasoning. If you wish, you can add some chopped bacon and mushrooms to the vegetables before browning them.

If the sauce is not thick enough, thicken it further with a little cornflour mixed with cold water.

White or béchamel sauce

450 ml	*milk*	*¾ pint*
one	*small onion*	*one*
four	*peppercorns*	*four*
	salt, nutmeg	
25 g	*butter*	*1 oz*
25 g	*flour*	*1 oz*

(Although this white sauce can be made without flavouring the milk first, this does improve the taste.) Bring the milk, with the onion and seasonings, to simmering point and leave it off the heat for 5–10 minutes, so that the flavours can be absorbed.

Make a white roux (page 217) and blend in the milk through a strainer, a little at a time. Reheat the sauce, stirring continuously while it thickens and comes to the boil. Leave it to simmer for 5–10 minutes to ensure that the flour is properly cooked. Check the seasoning.

If the sauce is to stand and be reheated later, spread a piece of buttered grease-proof paper with a hole in the middle over the surface. When you lift off the paper, the skin will come with it. Allow 70–150 ml (2½–5 fl oz) of sauce per person.

Sauce diable

Serve the sauce hot or cold, with roast meat, steaks or hamburgers, or even sausages or meat-balls.

two	*shallots*	*two*
	pepper	
100 ml	*dry white wine*	*3 fl oz*
300 ml	*brown sauce (page 180) or* *quick brown sauce (page 181)*	*½ pint*
one	*dash of Worcestershire sauce*	*one*
one	*dash of Tabasco*	*one*

Put the chopped shallots in a pan with some freshly-ground pepper and the wine. Boil until the wine has almost evaporated. Add the brown sauce, the Worcestershire sauce and the Tabasco. Stir well and cook for five minutes.

Savoury cherry sauce

Serve the sauce with duck, turkey or chicken. It is also good with roast veal. Dry-frozen cherries are excellent for this recipe.

25 g	butter	1 oz
one	small onion	one
one	small carrot	one
half	stick of celery	half
25 g	flour	1 oz
450 ml	chicken stock (page 215)	3/4 pint
150 ml	red wine	1/4 pint
	salt, pepper	
225 g	cooked or tinned cherries	1/2 lb
50 ml	cherry brandy	2 fl oz
25 ml	brandy	1 fl oz

Melt the butter and add the finely-chopped vegetables. Cook them for a few minutes before adding the flour. Stir it in well and cook it until it is nut-brown in colour. Add the stock, slowly, stirring constantly, then the wine, salt and pepper. Cook the sauce, covered, over a gentle heat for 30 minutes. Strain it through a fine sieve and return it to the pan. Add the cherries and their juice, the cherry brandy and the brandy. Reheat the sauce.

Madeira or port sauce

Serve the sauces with tongue, veal, steaks, cold meats, turkey fillets or sausages.

As a base use either the brown sauce on page 180 or the quick brown sauce on page 181.

To 300 ml (1/2 pint) of brown sauce, add 100 ml (3 fl oz) of madeira or port. Warm through and use as required.

Sweet-and-sour sauce

This is an Italian rather than a Chinese recipe. Serve the sauce with ham or tongue, poultry or sausages.

25 g	raisins	1 oz
25 g	sugar	1 oz
one 15 ml spoon	white wine vinegar	1 tablesp
150 ml	dry white wine	¼ pint
one 15 ml spoon	chopped shallot	1 tablesp
300 ml	brown sauce (page 180) or quick brown sauce (page 181)	½ pint

Soak the raisins in boiling water for five minutes. Heat the sugar and the vinegar in a heavy pan until the liquid starts to bubble. Add the wine and the chopped shallot, and continue to boil until the liquid is reduced to about two spoonsful. Strain the raisins. Add the brown sauce and raisins to the reduced liquid. Warm the sauce, stirring constantly. Taste it and, if necessary, add more sugar or vinegar.

White wine sauce

Serve the sauce with fish, white meat or poultry.

one	onion	one
50 g	butter	2 oz
25 g	flour	1 oz
150 ml	dry white wine	¼ pint
one	egg yolk	one
100 ml	single cream	3 fl oz
50 ml	water (see below)	2 fl oz
	salt, pepper	

Soften the finely-chopped onion in the butter. Add the flour and mix to a smooth paste. Slowly add the wine, stirring constantly. Cover the pan and cook the sauce for five minutes. Mix the egg yolk and cream in a bowl and add the sauce, a little at a time. Return the sauce to the pan, warm it through gently, adding a little water if it is too thick. Season well.

Mushroom sauce

This rich and creamy sauce is good enough to eat on its own as well as with hot or cold veal, chicken, pork or turkey. If you care to make it with double the quantity of mushrooms you will find yourself with an excellent first course. And if there is any left over, dilute it with stock to make a delicious soup.

110 g	button mushrooms	1/4 lb
40 g	butter	1 1/2 oz
40 g	flour	1 1/2 oz
300 ml	chicken stock (page 215)	1/2 pint
150 ml	white wine	1/4 pint
	grated nutmeg	
	salt, pepper	
100 ml	single cream	3 fl oz
one	egg yolk	one

Cook the thinly-sliced mushrooms in the melted butter until they are soft. Remove the pan from the heat and stir in the flour. Add the chicken stock, stirring continuously, and return the pan to the heat. Add the wine, a little nutmeg, salt and pepper. Cook over a gentle heat until the sauce thickens, stirring all the time.

Mix the cream with the egg yolk in a bowl and add the hot sauce, a little at a time, beating constantly. Return the cream mixture to the pan and warm it through over a very low heat.

Red wine sauce

Serve the sauce with hot or cold roast meat, hamburgers or poultry, or as part of a selection of sauces for fondue bourguignonne.

one 15 ml spoon	chopped shallot	1 tablesp
	butter	
200 ml	full-bodied red wine	7 fl oz
one 5 ml spoon	fresh thyme	1 teasp
	(or half quantity dried)	
	salt, pepper	
150 ml	beef stock (page 214)	¼ pint
15 g	butter	½ oz
one 15 ml spoon	flour	1 tablesp
one 5 ml spoon	lemon juice	1 teasp

Soften the finely-chopped shallot in a little butter. Add the wine, thyme, salt and pepper and cook it over a high heat until the liquid is reduced to a third. Add the stock. Make a beurre manié with the butter and flour (page 216). Add this, a little at a time, to the liquid, stirring constantly. Bring the sauce to the boil and cook it until it has thickened. Correct the seasoning. Sieve the sauce before adding the lemon juice.

Sauce lyonnaise

Serve the sauce with cold meats, steaks, hamburgers or roast meat.

three	large onions	three
two 15 ml spoons	butter	2 tablesp
two 15 ml spoons	flour	2 tablesp
125 ml	dry white wine	4 fl oz
50 ml	wine vinegar	2 fl oz
225 ml	beef stock (page 214)	8 fl oz
one 15 ml spoon	tomato puree	1 tablesp
	salt, pepper	

Soften the finely-chopped onions in hot butter until they are golden. Add the flour and stir well. Pour in the wine and vinegar, stirring constantly. Bring the sauce to the boil. Add the stock, tomato puree, salt and pepper. Simmer, uncovered, for ten minutes.

Savoury cider sauce

Serve the sauce with fish, white meat, poultry or green vegetables.

one	small onion	one
25 g	butter	1 oz
one 15 ml spoon	flour	1 tablesp
200–300 ml	dry cider	7–10 fl oz
	grated nutmeg	
	ground cinnamon	
150 ml	single cream	¼ pint
one 5 ml spoon	lemon juice	1 teasp
	salt, pepper	

Soften the finely-chopped onion in the butter. Add the flour and stir it well to make a smooth paste. Slowly add the cider, stirring, until you have the desired thickness. About 200 ml (7 fl oz) will make a fairly thick sauce – use more if you wish. Add a little nutmeg and cinnamon. Stir in the cream and lemon juice and season to taste.

Tomato sauce

Serve the sauce with veal, pork or poultry. If you use fish stock instead of the meat one you can also serve it with poached fish.

one	small onion	one
one 15 ml spoon	olive oil	1 tablesp
400 g	tinned tomatoes	14 oz
	basil (fresh if possible)	
	salt, pepper	
one 15 ml spoon	tomato puree	1 tablesp
150 ml	beef or veal stock (page 214)	¼ pint
one	pinch of sugar	one
one	sliver of lemon rind	one
100 ml	dry vermouth	3 fl oz

Soften the finely-chopped onion in the oil. Add all the remaining ingredients except the vermouth. Bring the sauce to the boil, and simmer it, covered, for 20 minutes. Sieve it, stir in the vermouth, and reheat gently.

Sherry cream sauce

You can adapt this sauce to go with fish as well as hot or cold veal, chicken, turkey or ham by changing the chopped ham to one 15 ml (table) spoonful of chopped anchovies.

40 g	*butter*	*1½ oz*
25 g	*flour*	*1 oz*
450 ml	*milk*	*¾ pint*
one 15 ml spoon	*chopped shallot*	*1 tablesp*
two 15 ml spoons	*chopped ham*	*2 tablesp*
two 15 ml spoons	*tomato puree*	*2 tablesp*
one 15 ml spoon	*lemon juice*	*1 tablesp*
	salt, pepper	
three 15 ml spoons	*dry sherry*	*3 tablesp*
one 15 ml spoon	*single cream*	*1 tablesp*

Melt the butter, remove the pan from the heat and stir in the flour. Add the milk, stirring continuously until the sauce is smooth. Return the pan to the heat and continue cooking until the sauce is thick. Add the finely-chopped shallot and ham, the tomato puree, lemon juice, salt and pepper. Cook the sauce for five minutes.

Stir in the sherry and cream and warm the sauce.

Sauce béarnaise

Don't be disheartened if your first attempts at this most delectable sauce end in disaster. You are in good company. It can be rescued quite miraculously, and even a curdled béarnaise is worth using, though not for V.I.P. guests. Serve it with roast or grilled meats and vegetables.

one 15 ml spoon	chopped shallot	1 tablesp
two 15 ml spoons	wine vinegar	2 tablesp
125 ml	dry white wine	4 fl oz
two 5 ml spoons	fresh tarragon (or half quantity dried)	2 teasp
two 15 ml spoons	cold water	2 tablesp
two	egg yolks	two
175 g	butter	6 oz
	salt, pepper	
one 5 ml spoon	chopped parsley	1 teasp

Put the finely-chopped shallot into a pan with the vinegar, the wine and half the tarragon. Bring the mixture to the boil and cook it over a high heat until the liquid has evaporated. Remove the pan from the heat and add the cold water.

Add the beaten egg yolks to the pan, whisking constantly. Return the pan to a very low heat, stirring constantly until the sauce thickens. Keep an eye on it all the time as the yolks will coagulate if the heat is too high.

Melt the butter carefully in another pan and add it to the yolk mixture, drop by drop, whisking the mixture all the time. When all the butter is incorporated, remove the pan from the heat. Season the sauce, stir in the chopped parsley and remaining tarragon, and serve it in a warmed sauce-boat.

You can make this a little in advance and keep it warm over hot – but not boiling – water. Stir the sauce occasionally. If it curdles, either while the butter is being added or when it is being kept warm, put two spoonsful of cold water into a clean bowl and beat in the curdled sauce, drop by drop. It will emulsify, as if by magic.

Beurre blanc

In the Loire, where this exquisite pale, creamy sauce comes from, you might expect to eat it with salmon or pike. Don't wait to catch these fish – the humbler cod or haddock are ideal excuses for the sauce. It is a tricky task to make beurre blanc since the butter should not over-heat. It should be served not hot, but lukewarm.

150 ml	dry white wine	¼ pint
one	shallot	one
225 g	unsalted butter	½ lb
	salt, pepper	

Put the wine and the finely-chopped shallot into a pan and bring the mixture to the boil. Cook it over a high heat until the liquid has almost evaporated. Reduce the heat as low as possible.

Have the chilled butter already cut into small pieces. Using a wire whisk, add the butter to the pan a piece at a time. Whisk it in well and before it dissolves add another piece of butter. Keep the heat very, very low at all times. If the butter starts to oil, plunge the pan immediately into a basin of cold water.

When all the butter is incorporated, add a little salt and freshly-ground pepper. Put the sauce into a warmed sauce-boat and serve it immediately.

Red wine marinade

This marinade is suitable for beef or lamb, for barbecuing or indoor cooking.

one	medium-sized onion	one
one	clove of garlic	one
one	bouquet garni (page 216)	one
200 ml	red wine	7 fl oz
two 15 ml spoons	oil	2 tablesp
	salt, pepper	

Slice the onion, crush the garlic and add them to the remaining ingredients. Mix everything together well and pour over the meat. Leave for a minimum of two hours before cooking as required.

Marinade for barbecuing

This marinade is suitable for lamb, chicken, pork spare ribs or chops. You can grill them or cook them in the oven as you prefer.

175 ml	soy sauce	6 fl oz
50 ml	tomato ketchup	2 fl oz
two 15 ml spoons	brown sugar or honey	2 tablesp
125 ml	dry sherry	4 fl oz
one	small onion	one
one	clove of garlic	one
one	lemon	one

Combine the soy sauce, ketchup, sugar and sherry in a liquidiser. Add the chopped onion, crushed garlic and the juice of the lemon with a little grated rind. Liquidise everything well to make a smooth mixture. Pour the marinade over the meat and leave it to marinate for a minimum of two hours. Drain it well before cooking.

Sweet wine sauce

This Austrian sauce is rather like a thick mulled wine. It can be served hot or cold, with ice-cream, steamed puddings, crêpes, and omelettes. It is even delicious with noodles.

200 ml	red wine	7 fl oz
two	cloves	two
half	stick of cinnamon	half
one	lemon	one
75 g	sugar	3 oz
one 15 ml spoon	cornflour	1 tablesp
two 15 ml spoons	water	2 tablesp
two 15 ml spoons	redcurrant jelly	2 tablesp

Combine in a pan the wine, the cloves, the cinnamon, the juice and a little grated rind of the lemon, and the sugar, and cook the mixture over a gentle heat for 20 minutes. Sieve the sauce into a clean pan, add the cornflour, mixed with the water to a smooth paste. Cook the sauce over a gentle heat, stirring until it thickens. Add the redcurrant jelly and stir the sauce until the jelly has dissolved.

Austrian punch sauce

Serve the sauce hot or cold with soft fruit, stewed fruit or fruit pies.

one 15 ml spoon	cornflour	1 tablesp
225 ml	fruity white wine	8 fl oz
two	egg yolks	two
one	lemon	one
one 15 ml spoon (approx.)	sugar	1 tablesp (approx.)
two 5 ml spoons	brandy	2 teasp

Mix the cornflour with a little wine to a smooth paste. Combine this mixture with the rest of the wine in a saucepan, together with the egg yolks, the juice of the lemon and a little grated rind, and the sugar. Blend everything with an egg whisk and continue whisking the mixture over a gentle heat until it is thick and foaming. Take care not to let it get too hot. Stir in the brandy, and either serve the sauce at once or allow it to cool.

Brandy sauce

Serve the sauce hot, with ice-cream, pancakes, waffles or banana splits.

50 g	butter	2 oz
75 g	sugar	3 oz
two 15 ml spoons	golden syrup	2 tablesp
100 ml	single cream	3 fl oz
one	pinch of salt	one
three 15 ml spoons	brandy	3 tablesp

Melt the butter in a small saucepan and add the sugar, syrup, cream and salt. Stir the sauce and bring it to the boil. Reduce the heat, cover the pan, and simmer it for two minutes. Add the brandy and simmer the sauce for a further two minutes.

Brandy butter

Although this is usually served only with Christmas pudding, it seems too good to relegate to a once-yearly appearance. It is good with hot mince pies, apple pie and steamed puddings. It will freeze well, or keep in the refrigerator for up to three weeks.

175 g	*unsalted butter*	*6 oz*
175 g	*icing sugar*	*6 oz*
three 15 ml spoons	*brandy*	*3 tablesp*

Cream the butter to soften it. Sieve the sugar onto it and beat the mixture until it is smooth. Add the brandy and beat again until the mixture is white and fluffy.

Refrigerate the brandy butter, covered, until it is required.

Substitute rum for the brandy and soft brown sugar for the icing sugar, if you prefer rum butter.

Drinks

There are fashions in drinks as in so many other areas of life. One year everyone is asking for cocktails and the next we are all sipping a glass of white wine as an aperitif. Whether you follow the trends – or set your own – it is useful to have a few ideas up your sleeve, and it is worth remembering that for parties you are saving yourself a lot of trouble if you stick to one drink throughout the evening. A mulled wine, cider or beer might be just right for a cold winter's night, and their chilled cousins equally suitable for the scorching summer's eve we all pray for when planning a summer party. If these do not appeal, there are literally thousands of cocktails, with new ones always being created by adventurous barmen around the globe. This is where your own imagination can flourish, for there seems to be no limit to the often rather extraordinary combinations which can be served as cocktails. Liqueurs, often served 'neat', can be altered, enhanced and varied in all sorts of ways.

The wine table (page 14) and the liqueurs and spirits table (page 15) will help you make valid substitutions if one of the required ingredients is missing.

So armed with a measure, a punch-bowl and a cocktail-shaker, you are all set to enter for the Barperson of the Year competition.

Cocktails

The many classic cocktails can be found in recipe collections, and any avid cocktail-shaker might wish to acquire the appropriate books. Recipes are also often to be found on leaflets issued by producers and shippers of liqueurs and spirits. I have limited my list to some more recent inventions. The quantities given are for one drink, and the measure you use will determine the size of the drink. In all cases the ingredients should be mixed or shaken together and served very cold.

ACACIA
⅔ gin; ⅓ Bénédictine; one dash of kirsch

CARUSO
⅓ Noilly Prat; ⅓ gin; ⅓ Pippermint

DEAUVILLE
¼ calvados; ¼ brandy; ¼ Cointreau; ¼ fresh lemon juice

EPISCOPAL
⅓ Yellow Chartreuse; ⅔ Green Chartreuse

HAMLET
½ Cherry Heering; ½ Aalborg Akvavit

MAID OF ERIN
⅓ Royal Mint-Chocolate Liqueur; ⅓ cream; ⅓ brandy

NEGRONI
⅓ dry gin; ⅓ sweet vermouth; ⅓ Campari; ice cubes; 1 slice of orange

PEACE TREATY
½ Sabra; ½ vodka; ice cubes

RED LION
⅓ dry gin; ⅓ Grand Marnier; ⅓ orange juice; 1 dash of lemon juice

ROYAL DUTCH
¾ Nassau Orange Liqueur; ¼ cognac

WATERLOO
⅕ Mandarine Napoléon; ⅕ light rum; ⅗ orange juice; one 5 ml (tea) spoon sugar

Other drinks

Included here are concoctions which do not conveniently come under the heading of cocktails, although they are certainly mixtures of various different liquids.

Black Velvet

½ Guinness; ½ champagne

Buck's Fizz

A lovely morning drink, pre-breakfast or brunch.

½ chilled orange juice; ½ champagne or sparkling wine

Pour the champagne onto the orange juice.

Cuba Libre

Half a lime; ice; 50 ml (2 fl oz) rum; 200 ml (7 fl oz) cola

Put the juice of the lime in a tall glass with a little rind. Add the ice and rum and fill the glass with cola.

Eggnog (12 glasses approx.)

A traditional American drink for a New Year's Day party.

6 eggs; 75 g (3 oz) caster sugar; 225 ml (8 fl oz) brandy; 600 ml
(1 pint) milk; 600 ml (1 pint) whipping cream; grated nutmeg

Beat the egg yolks with the sugar until they are thick and creamy. Continue beating as
you add the brandy. Chill this mixture for two hours. Stir the milk into the yolk mixture
and gently fold in the cream. Beat the whites until they are stiff and fold them into the
nog. Chill again for an hour or more. Serve with a little grated nutmeg sprinkled over
each glass.

Vary the flavour by using half brandy and half bourbon.

Flips

These can be made using brandy, rum, whisky, port, sherry or claret.

For a brandy flip: one 5 ml (tea) spoon sugar; 1 egg; 50 ml (2 fl oz) brandy; ice; grated
nutmeg

Shake the sugar, egg and brandy together with the ice. Strain it into a glass and add a
little grated nutmeg.

Harvey Wallbanger

Ice; 1 measure of vodka; 4 measures of orange juice; half a measure of Galliano

Fill a tall glass with ice, and pour in the vodka and orange juice. Float the Galliano on
top.

Hot gin sling

One 5 ml (tea) spoon sugar; 50 ml (2 fl oz) gin; 25 ml (1 fl oz) lemon juice; hot water; grated nutmeg

Mix the sugar, gin and lemon juice in a tall glass. Fill the glass with hot water. Sprinkle a little grated nutmeg on top.

Hot toddy

1 pinch of sugar; 1 strip of lemon peel; 1 clove; 1 small piece of cinnamon; 100 ml (3 fl oz) whisky; boiling water

Warm a mug. Place all the ingredients in the mug, filling it up with the boiling water.

Kir

1 glass dry white wine (preferably burgundy). Add Crème de Cassis to taste – about a 5 ml (tea) spoon – and stir well. Serve well chilled.

A Kir Royale is similar to Kir, with champagne instead of the still wine.

Liqueurs frappés

Any liqueur poured over crushed ice. An essential part of this drink is a straw to drink it through.

Milk shakes

200 ml (7 fl oz) cold milk; 1 generous scoop of vanilla ice-cream; 1 liqueur glass of the chosen liqueur

Blend all the ingredients together for 30 seconds.

Piña Pernod

25 ml (1 fl oz) Pernod; ice cubes; 175 ml (6 fl oz) pineapple juice

Pour the Pernod over the ice cubes and add the fruit juice.

Pink Pussy

25 ml (1 fl oz) Campari; 15 ml (½ fl oz) peach brandy; 125 ml (4 fl oz) bitter lemon; ice; 1 slice of orange

Mix together everything except the orange in a tall glass. Add the orange slice.

Remus Fizz (3 glasses)

1 cup crushed ice; 125 ml (4 fl oz) orange juice; 100 ml (3 fl oz) single cream; 2 dashes orange flower water; 100 ml (3 fl oz) gin; two 5 ml (tea) spoons sugar; 1 egg; ground cinnamon or grated nutmeg

Liquidise everything except the spice. Serve in chilled glasses with cinnamon or nutmeg on top.

Pousse-Café

Considerable skill is involved in the making of this drink. The different liqueurs must remain in separate layers, one above the other. In order to achieve this effect you must pour the liqueurs slowly over the back of a spoon, which is held touching the edge of the glass. Follow the order given, as it is the difference in densities which prevents the mingling of the ingredients.

You need equal quantities of each; therefore, using five different liqueurs and the syrupy grenadine, you will want one-sixth measure of each:
grenadine; maraschino; green crème de menthe; crème de violette; Chartreuse; brandy

Rum tea

40 ml (1½ fl oz) rum; a glass of iced tea

Prairie Oyster

And to help you sober up after all the preceding drinks, try a pick-me-up.

One 5 ml (tea) spoon Worcestershire sauce; one 5 ml (tea) spoon tomato ketchup;
1 egg yolk; 2 dashes of vinegar and a dash of pepper

Pour the Worcestershire sauce and ketchup into a glass. Carefully drop the egg yolk in without breaking it. Pour over the vinegar and add the pepper.

Liqueur coffee

Many restaurants feature their own particular liqueur coffee, the most famous versions being Irish or Gaelic. The same principle can be applied to any liqueur and conjuring up your own version makes an amusing finale to an evening. The list I give is a 'classic' one, but anything goes. The method and basic ingredients are the same for all.

One 5 ml (tea) spoon sugar; 40 ml (1½ fl oz) Irish whiskey (or whatever you choose); 150 ml (¼ pint) strong black coffee (hot); one 15 ml (table) spoon whipped cream

Put the sugar and whiskey into a warmed glass. Add the coffee and stir it to dissolve the sugar. Float the cream on top over the back of a teaspoon.

Alpine Coffee: with Enzian liqueur or spirit
Belgian Coffee: Elixir d'Anvers
Calypso Coffee: Tia Maria
Caribbean Coffee: rum
Dutch Coffee: genever
French (or Royal) Coffee: cognac
German Coffee: kirsch
Italian (or Witches') Coffee: Strega
Mexican Coffee: Kahlùa
Monks' Coffee: Bénédictine or Chartreuse
Normandy Coffee: calvados
Prince Charles Coffee: Drambuie
Royal Mint Coffee: Royal Mint-Chocolate
Russian Coffee: vodka
Scandinavian Coffee: aquavit
Scotch Coffee: Scotch whisky
Westphalian Coffee: Steinhäger

Cold wine cups

On a hot summer's evening there is nothing nicer than a cool, refreshing wine cup. You need not use expensive wines for these recipes and the beauty of them for a party is their infinite expandability. Start off with the given mixture and add another bottle of wine, cider, or whatever, to keep it going throughout the evening. Don't wait for a party in order to enjoy these drinks, which can also be scaled down to suit your numbers.

Claret cup (10 glasses approx.)

75 g (3 oz) sugar; 150 ml (¼ pint) water; 2 oranges; 2 lemons; 2 bottles claret; ice; soda water; slices of cucumber, apple or orange; sprigs of mint

Boil the sugar and water with the rind of the oranges and lemons. Combine the juice of the fruit with this syrup and let it cool. Pour the claret into a large bowl and add the cooled syrup and the ice. Just before serving add the soda water and float the slices of cucumber, fruit and mint on top.

German Bowle (30 glasses approx.)

450 g (1 lb) tinned pineapple *or* fresh strawberries *or* ripe sliced peaches; 3 bottles German wine; ice; 1 bottle sparkling wine *or* ½ bottle each sparkling wine and soda; sugar to taste

Put the selected fruit into a large bowl and add the still wine. Refrigerate it for one hour. Add the ice cubes and sparkling wine, and sugar to taste. Serve it very cold.

Rhine Sparkler (25 glasses approx.)

1 melon or other fresh fruit; sugar to taste; 3 bottles Rhine wine; 1 bottle sparkling wine; liqueur glass of brandy; ice; fruit to decorate if you wish

Cube the melon or slice any other fruit and place it in a large bowl with the sugar and the still wine. Refrigerate it for one hour and add the sparkling wine and other ingredients.

Safari cup (35–40 glasses approx.)

2 bottles sweet white wine; 1 litre (1¾ pints) still draught cider; ⅕ bottle of brandy;

1 bottle orange and passion-fruit squash; 1 lemon (sliced); 1 orange (sliced); 1 apple (sliced); 2 large bottles lemonade

Mix all the ingredients together except the lemonade. Refrigerate the mixture for several hours. Add the lemonade just before serving.

Sangria (24 glasses approx.)

2 bottles red wine; sliced apples, oranges, lemons and peaches; 2 large bottles soda water; ice

Add the wine to the fruit in a large bowl and refrigerate it for at least one hour. Add the soda water and ice immediately before serving. Add a measure of brandy if you wish to make the sangria more 'punchy'.

Hot wine punches

The smell alone of mulled wine is enough to make one feel warm and cossetted, with the heady aroma of spices mingled with the wine. Serve your mull hot, but not boiling, since all the alcohol would evaporate. Remember to put spoons in the glasses before pouring in the hot wine to prevent their cracking. Use inexpensive wines for mulling – for 'claret' substitute a similar type of wine.

Port and lemon mull (12 glasses approx.)

This mull is sometimes known as 'The Bishop'.

8 cloves; 2 lemons; 1 bottle port; 600 ml (1 pint) boiling water; 1 small stick of cinnamon; 1 pinch of grated nutmeg; 50 g (2 oz) lump sugar

Stick the cloves into one of the lemons and put it on a plate in the oven to warm for 15 minutes. Pour the port into a saucepan and bring it almost to the boil. Add the boiling water to the pan, along with the cinnamon, nutmeg and baked lemon. Rub the lumps of sugar on the rind of the other lemon and put the sugar into a bowl. Squeeze the juice of the lemon over the sugar and add this to the hot wine. Serve hot.

Dr Johnson's Choice (25 glasses approx.)

This was a popular 18th-century recipe.

1 litre (1¾ pints) claret; 1 orange; 12 lumps of sugar; 6 cloves; 600 ml (1 pint) boiling water; 150 ml (¼ pint) brandy; grated nutmeg

Pour the claret into a saucepan and add the sliced orange, sugar and cloves. Bring the mixture almost to the boil and add the boiling water and the brandy. Pour the mull into warmed glasses and sprinkle a little nutmeg over each one.

Mulled claret (8 glasses approx.)

12 cloves; 1 pinch of grated nutmeg; 150 ml (¼ pint) water; 1 bottle claret; 150 ml (¼ pint) port; one 15 ml (table) spoon sugar; lemon rind

Put the spices into a saucepan with the water and simmer it gently for half an hour. Strain the spiced water into another pan and add the claret, port and sugar. Bring this mixture almost to the boil. Serve it very hot, with thin slices of lemon rind. A small stick of cinnamon can be used either with, or instead of, the lemon rind.

Beer punches

Some charming traditions are associated with mulled ales, together with equally delightful names. The Brewers Society told me never to do more than warm the drink and to have ready a tray of salt cellars or other small dishes containing ginger, nutmeg and cinnamon (all powdered or ground), lemon peel and a few cloves. Put a salt spoon with each salt cellar so that the drinkers can take small quantities of the spices and sprinkle them on top of the ale to suit their own taste. Serve punch in punch glasses (which have handles) or small mugs.

Beer flip (8 glasses approx.)

This is an old English drink served to bell-ringers after a long peal. The instructions are to serve it swiftly while hot, with the echo of the bells still ringing.

8 eggs; two 15 ml (table) spoons sugar; 50 ml (2 fl oz) orange juice; 1 litre (1¾ pints) strong ale; one 5 ml (tea) spoon ground mixed spices

Separate the eggs and beat the yolks with the sugar and orange juice. Whip the whites until they are stiff. Warm the beer and pour it over the yolks. Pour it back and forth from a height between two containers so that it becomes frothy. Fold in the beaten whites. Sprinkle the spices on before serving.

Jesus College, Oxford, Wassail Bowl (12 glasses approx.)

The bowl referred to was a silver-gilt bowl of 1722 presented to the college by Sir Watkin Wynne. This punch is known in Oxford as 'Swig'.

225 g (½ lb) brown sugar; 3.5 litres (6 pints) beer; grated nutmeg; ground ginger; 450 ml (¾ pint) sherry; sugar to taste; 5 slices of thin toast

Put the sugar into a large bowl. Warm half of the beer and pour it over the sugar. Sprinkle over the spices. Add the sherry and the remaining beer. Stir the mixture and sweeten it to taste. Let it stand for two to three hours. Just before serving, float the slices of toast on top of the beer. Sometimes two or three slices of lemon are added.

Lamb's Wool (6 glasses approx.)

This is a wassail bowl traditionally served on November 1st, the Day of the Apple Fruit or La Mas Ubal, which was anglicised in Norman times to Lamasool and later Lambswool. It is also served in Ireland on Holy Eve, the night before All Saints' Day.

6 roasted cooking apples; sugar to taste; grated nutmeg; ground ginger; 1.25 litres (2 pints) strong ale

Mix the pulp of the roasted apples (or the equivalent amount of apple sauce) with sugar to taste. Sprinkle over some grated nutmeg and ground ginger. Warm the ale and stir it into the apple mixture. Sweet cakes may be served floating in the mull.

Oxford Nightcap (12 glasses approx.)

Known as a Grace cup, because it was offered to retiring or departing guests, this was published in a book of *Oxford Nightcaps* in 1835.

1 lemon; 1 litre (1¾ pints) strong ale; 1 bottle dry white wine; grated nutmeg; sugar to taste; 4 slices of toast

Peel the lemon and cut it into thin slices. Put them into a jug or bowl and add the ale and wine. Sprinkle some grated nutmeg onto it, sweeten to taste, and stir until the sugar is dissolved. Add four slices of toast and let the drink stand for two hours. Strain it off into another bowl (or Grace Cup if you have one).

Cider drinks

Punches and mulls of cider make excellent party drinks, easy on the purse and – the milder ones at least – suitable for younger guests.

Mulled cider punch (12 glasses)

1 orange; 1 lemon; 12 cloves; 150 ml (¼ pint) water; 1 piece of cinnamon; 1 piece of root ginger; 50 g (1 oz) brown sugar; 3 litres (5 pints) cider

Spike the orange and lemon with the cloves. Bake in a moderate oven (180°C, 350°F, mark 4) for 20 minutes. Put the water, cinnamon, ginger and sugar into a large pan. Stir the mixture over medium heat until the sugar has dissolved. Add the orange, lemon and cider. Warm the punch over a gentle heat but do not allow it to boil. You can serve this chilled if you wish.

Cider toddy (8 glasses)

1.75 litres (3 pints) medium-dry cider; grated nutmeg; ground ginger; sugar to taste; eight 15 ml (table) spoons calvados; four 15 ml (table) spoons double cream

Heat the cider gently in a large pan with the spices and sugar, but do not allow it to boil. Stir in the calvados. Pour the toddy into eight glasses (with a spoon in each). Float a little cream on top of each glass.

Cider sangria (10 glasses approx.)

1 litre (1¾ pints) dry or medium-dry cider; 300 ml (½ pint) orange juice; 1 bottle red wine; three 15 ml (table) spoons brandy; 1 apple; 1 orange; 1 lemon; cherries; strawberries; 300 ml (½ pint) soda water; ice

Mix everything together in a large bowl, except for the soda and ice. Leave the mixture in a cold place for a few hours. Just before serving add the soda and ice.

Evening Glory (per person)

25 ml (1 fl oz) whisky; one 15 ml (table) spoon crushed ice; 1 strip lemon peel; 175 ml (6 fl oz) dry cider

Mix everything together thoroughly in a jug and pour it into a glass.

Cider Apple Jack (per person)

Two 15 ml (table) spoons calvados; one 15 ml (table) spoon crushed ice; 2 thin slices of apple; 1 maraschino cherry; 175 ml (6 fl oz) dry cider

Mix everything together thoroughly in a jug and pour it into a glass.

Basic recipes and definitions

Throughout the book, cross-references are given for basic stocks, pastries, sauces, and so on, as well as for commonly-used culinary terms. Most cookery books contain some of these, but it is convenient to have them all to hand in the book you are actually using. Several are reprinted here from the *Good Food Guide*'s previous cookery books.

Shortcrust pastry/pâte brisée (160 g/6 oz)

110 g	*flour*	*¼ lb*
half 5 ml spoon	*salt*	*½ teasp*
50 g	*butter*	*2 oz*
two 15 ml spoons	*cold water (approx.)*	*2 tablesp*

Sift the flour and salt into a bowl. Cut up the butter and crumble it into the flour with the fingertips or a wire pastry mixer. Mix in enough cold water with a knife to make a firm dough, and roll it into a ball. On a floured board, stretch out the pastry bit by bit with the heel of the palm, then gather it up again into a ball. Repeat this process, dust the pastry with a little flour and wrap it in buttered paper or foil. Refrigerate it for up to two hours to firm.

To line a flan case, roll out the pastry on a floured board to the thickness of 2.5–5 mm (⅛-¼ inch) and about 5 cm (2 inches) bigger than the flan case. Grease the case and lay the pastry gently in it, pressing it down to fit the bottom and sides. Ease a little extra down the sides before cutting off the excess. Prick the bottom lightly. Leave it to rest in a cool place for 30 minutes, to prevent its shrinking during cooking.

If the pastry case is to be cooked empty or 'blind', line it with a piece of foil or grease-proof paper weighted with dry beans and bake it on a baking-sheet for ten minutes at 200°C (400°F, mark 6). Remove the paper and put the case back in the oven for another 7–10 minutes until it is lightly browned. Remove the pastry shell from its tin and cool it on a rack. (Using a flan ring, rather than a case, makes this operation very simple.)

Sweet shortcrust pastry/pâte sucrée (225 g/½ lb)

110 g	*flour*	*¼ lb*
half 5 ml spoon	*salt*	*½ teasp*
50 g	*sugar*	*2 oz*
50 g	*softened butter*	*2 oz*
one	*egg yolk*	*one*

Sift the flour and salt into a bowl and make a well in the centre for the other ingredients. Mix them together with the fingertips and gradually draw the flour into them until it is all incorporated. Knead the pastry lightly until it is smooth, flour and wrap it, and put it in the refrigerator to chill for up to two hours.

Puff pastry/pâte feuilletée (450 g /1 lb)

225 g	*strong flour*	*½ lb*
half 5 ml spoon	*salt*	*½ teasp*
225 g	*unsalted butter*	*½ lb*
one	*squeeze of lemon*	*one*

The coolest possible conditions, utensils and ingredients are essential when preparing this kind of pastry, which contains a high proportion of fat; on the other hand, it is then baked in a really hot oven so that the air trapped between the layers will quickly expand and puff it up.

Sift the flour and salt and rub in about 15 g (½ oz) of the butter. Make it into a fairly soft dough with about 100 ml (3–4 fl oz) of ice-cold water and a squeeze of lemon (the lemon strengthens the dough but too much liquid toughens it), and knead it well on a floured surface until it is smooth. Rest it for 15 minutes in the refrigerator.

Roll out the dough into an oblong roughly 30 cm by 10 (12 inches by 4). Flatten the remaining piece of butter – it should be slightly softened – into a rectangle about half the size, and place this on one half of the dough, or cut the butter in thin slices and place them evenly over half the surface of the dough. Fold the other half over and press the edges together with a rolling-pin or with the side of your hand. Turn the fold to one side and roll out the pastry again, with short, quick movements, into an oblong the size of the original one. Keep the pastry regular in shape with square corners and do not roll the pin over the edges or stretch the dough. Fold it into three and seal the edges to trap the air inside. Wrap the pastry in grease-proof paper and put it to rest in a really cool place or in the refrigerator for twenty minutes.

Repeat this turning, rolling, folding and resting operation five more times, always starting with the fold to the same side, and chilling between rollings.

Puff pastry can be made in quantity and frozen – it freezes very well. Prepare it up to, but not including, the last rolling. Bought puff pastry is an acceptable alternative but should be rolled out to a thickness of 2.5 mm (⅛ inch) as it rises very well.

Brandy-snaps

Brandy-snaps are a useful accompaniment to creamy sweets, which would seem to be a good reason to include the recipe, in spite of the miniscule amount of brandy used. They also happen to be great fun to make, though practice makes perfect, as in all matters culinary.

110 g	*unsalted butter*	*¼ lb*
110 g	*caster sugar*	*¼ lb*
110 g	*flour*	*¼ lb*
four 15 ml spoons	*golden syrup*	*4 tablesp*
two 5 ml spoons	*brandy*	*2 teasp*
half 5 ml spoon	*ground ginger*	*½ teasp*

Mix all the ingredients together in a bowl to a smooth paste and divide it into 15 g (½ oz) balls (about 24). It is worth being quite accurate as you then get biscuits of the same size. Place the balls very well apart on a greased tray and flatten them slightly. Bake them in a moderate oven (180°C, 350°F, mark 4) for about five minutes until they are golden brown in colour.

Cool them very slightly and while they are still warm, roll them round a wooden-spoon handle until they are set and crisp. It is as well to bake only one tray at a time. If they go hard before you have rolled them, put the tray back in the oven for a few seconds to soften them.

Store the brandy-snaps in an airtight container.

Crème pâtissière

Custard, ugh! But call it crème pâtissière and suddenly everyone loves it. It is certainly a most useful, if not essential, ingredient in many sweets and whether you choose to flavour it with vanilla, or any liqueur you can think of, it makes a most satisfactory sweet on its own.

450 ml	milk	¾ pint
75 g	vanilla sugar (page 218)	3 oz
four	egg yolks	four
25 g	flour	1 oz

Heat the milk with the sugar. Mix the egg yolks and the flour to a smooth paste and when the milk is beginning to boil, very slowly pour it onto the egg mixture, stirring all the time. Return the mixture to the pan and heat it gently, stirring constantly until it just comes to the boil. Remove the pan from the heat at once and stir in any flavouring required by the recipe. (If you are adding a liqueur, you may prefer to use plain rather than vanilla sugar.)

Beer batter

Beer makes batter surprisingly light. The beery flavour doesn't come through and the batter is suitable for sweet or savoury use.

110 g	flour	¼ lb
one	pinch of salt	one
two	eggs	two
300 ml	light ale	½ pint

Sieve the flour and salt. Separate the eggs and beat the yolks into the flour with a whisk. Stir in the ale and mix the batter until it is smooth. Leave it to rest for half an hour or more if possible. Just before you are ready to use the batter, gently fold the stiffly-beaten egg whites into it.

Stocks

I have elsewhere mentioned stock cubes as an alternative to home-made stock. I think it would be a pity to be put off making a recipe because you don't happen to have any home-made stock, and for that reason I suggest using good commercial stock cubes, with the proviso that you check the seasoning carefully since stock cubes tend to be very highly seasoned.

Beef stock

1 kg	beef or veal bones or part meat, part bones	2 lb
one	large carrot	one
one	onion	one
one	bouquet garni (page 216) with celery leaves	one
six	peppercorns	six

Brown the pieces of meat, bones and sliced vegetables for 30 minutes in a roasting-tin in a hot oven (220°C, 425°F, mark 7). Put them with the herbs and peppercorns into a large saucepan with enough cold water to cover them by at least 2.5 cm (one inch) – about two litres (3½ pints). Bring slowly to the boil, skim, and simmer very gently with the lid partly off for 4–5 hours. Skim off any scum as it rises. Strain the stock and leave it to stand to allow the fat to rise to the surface. Remove this with a spoon or absorbent paper, or leave the stock to get cold when the congealed fat can be easily removed. If strongly flavoured stock is required, reduce it by boiling before adding the seasoning.

Stock can be kept deep-frozen for several weeks; otherwise it must be re-boiled every day, or every few days if it is stored in the refrigerator.

For a white veal stock, use veal bones and veal, and omit the preliminary browning.

Chicken stock

one	boiling fowl with giblets (or portion, or carcase with trimmings plus 450 g [1 lb] giblets)	one
one	piece of chopped veal bone (optional) vegetables and herbs as for beef stock	one

Prepare as for beef stock but without the preliminary browning. Simmer for 2–3 hours. Chill the stock and remove the fat before use. If a whole fowl is being used, remove it from the stock after the first hour, carve off the breasts and use these for any dish calling for cooked chicken. Stock made from cooked meat only, such as the remains of a roast chicken, does not taste at all the same and might impart its distinctive flavour to a dish.

Fish stock

450–700 g	fish, fish bones and/or trimmings	1–1½ lb
one	onion	one
six	parsley stems	six
half	lemon	half
half 5 ml spoon	salt	½ teasp
eight	white peppercorns	eight
600 ml	water or water and dry white wine, mixed	1 pint

This can be used as the basis of a fish velouté sauce. Use less fish for a lighter stock for poaching fish. Prawn shells add flavour. The stock is delicate; for a heartier one add thyme or a bouquet garni (page 216), carrot or turnip, celery or mushroom trimmings.

Wash the fish and trimmings thoroughly in cold water. Break them into pieces and put them with the sliced onion, the parsley stems, the juice and rind of the half-lemon, the salt, pepper and water (or wine and water) in a large saucepan. Bring slowly to the boil, skim, reduce the heat, and simmer the stock slowly, partly covered, for 30 minutes. Strain it, and either use it at once or refrigerate it.

Stock syrup

| 450 g | sugar | 1 lb |
| 450 ml | water | ³/₄ pint |

Boil the sugar and water together for two minutes. Cool the syrup, bottle it, and refrigerate it. It will keep for a week or more.

Bain-marie

A shallow pan or dish half-filled with water near simmering point, in which are placed smaller dishes or pans containing pâté, for example, or eggs, or a sauce. The bain-marie can be used on top of the stove or in the oven, either to keep the contents hot or to cook them by indirect heat without danger of curdling or burning. An adaptation of the bain-marie is the double-boiler where the inner container is suspended *over* the simmering water.

Beurre manié

This is an uncooked mixture of butter and flour kneaded together and added to the liquid at the end of cooking in order to thicken it.

Mix to a paste equal quantities of softened butter and flour, then add it to the liquid in pieces the size of a sugar lump. Stir in each one off the heat until it has dissolved, and return the pan to the stove to allow the liquid to thicken.

Bouquet garni

A bundle of aromatic herbs used to add flavour to stocks, sauces or stews. It is composed of one or two parsley stalks, a bay leaf and a sprig of thyme. When other herbs or vegetables are required (such as celery leaves), these are usually specified.

Tie the herbs together with a long piece of cotton or string so that they can easily be removed at the end of the cooking. If dried herbs are being used, put them in a square of muslin and tie the ends together.

Duxelles

A preparation of minced mushroom and shallot or onion, cooked until it is dry, used for flavouring stuffings.

Chop 110 g (¼ lb) mushrooms very finely and wring them out in a cloth to dry them as much as possible. Fry them in a very little butter with two chopped shallots or half an onion until all the liquid has evaporated and the mixture is cooked. Season. The duxelles can be made in bulk, packed into a sealed container and refrigerated, or frozen.

Roux

A blend of roughly equal weights of butter and flour, first cooked together before the liquid is incorporated for a sauce. A roux can be described as white (for a béchamel), light brown, or brown (for a brown sauce).

Melt the butter gently in a saucepan, blend in the flour and stir over heat for a minute or two to cook the flour. If a light brown roux is required cook until it starts to turn a golden colour. For a brown roux, continue until it is nut-brown. (This can be done very easily by putting the pan in a hot oven for about ten minutes.)

Reduction

A sauce, stock or soup, can be thickened by boiling it steadily (uncovered) until the quantity of liquid is reduced through evaporation.

Vanilla sugar

Sugar which has absorbed the flavour of a vanilla pod, used in the making of sweet pastry, custard and fruit dishes.

Put one or two pieces of vanilla pod into a tightly-stoppered jar of caster sugar. After a few days the sugar will have become flavoured. The pieces of vanilla can be left in the jar which can be topped up with fresh sugar as required; the flavour will continue to be imparted for years.

Equivalent temperatures

Celsius	Fahrenheit	Gas mark
110°	225°	¼
120°	250°	½
140°	275°	1
150°	300°	2
160°	325°	3
180°	350°	4
190°	375°	5
200°	400°	6
220°	425°	7
230°	450°	8
240°	475°	9
260°	500°	–
270°	525°	–

Index of recipes

INDEX

Index of drinks